D1711391

CHASING JESUS

A startling, gut-level discovery and an unflinchingly honest journey to a surprising potential for peace of soul in troubled times

Jack Prohaska

A deeply spiritual epiphany involving the "Language of God" has profoundly affected my Christian life. This book is for those out there who, if their hearts and minds are open to it and they recognize it for what it is, might well have the same experience.

Author website: http://www.JAXLayMinistries.com;
facebook/JAX-Lay-Ministries

All artwork copyright © 2021 Brian J. Prohaska, Sr. Cover designed by Brian and Jack Prohaska.

Nun photo © (used for drawing) Content License Agreement obtained through iStock.

Disclaimer: Names have been changed to protect the identities of certain characters in the story.

Edited by Rachel L. M. Hall.

C. S. Lewis quotes provided courtesy C. S. Lewis Co.

Published 2021, BookBaby™.

FIRST EDITION

Print ISBN: 978-1-09834-866-3
eBook ISBN: 978-1-09834-867-0

Printed in the United States of America on SFI Certified paper.

CONTENTS

ENDORSEMENTS

"A masterpiece of Christian witness in a down-to-earth and easy read. The author uses subtle humor and creativity to share with the reader the serious struggle for God and Truth. The author is vulnerable before the reader, revealing the tension between his deep stirrings of faith and the existential confusion of his church-going experience. An honest and sincere indictment of modern-day churches, but with the eventual endorsement of the value of the Christian faith (churches included) in finding answers in our lives."

Father Alexander Lukashonok,
All Holy Spirit Orthodox Church,
Omaha, Nebraska

"I was moved by *Chasing Jesus*…it is a humorous, nearly indescribable journey that will relate to anyone who reads it. Jack's ability to narrate his path moves the reader in a manner rare among religious texts. Not a feel-good or a '*Kum ba yah*', this book is unique—an atypical Christian work that will touch persons of all faiths. I really wish I had read it earlier!"

Dr. Paul Nader, DSS, MMOAS, Adjunct Professor, Political Science, Midland University, Fremont, Nebraska

"I have known Mr. Prohaska since high school and admire his ability as a wordsmith. Here is a writer who looks at the Christian experience truly objectively, covering a great variety of things, seeding profound concepts with wit and common sense throughout. This is a unique book, the core of which is a surprising gift C. S. Lewis left us all. Lewis called it 'essential'—something for Christians of *all* persuasions."

Rev. John Shriver, BS and M.Ed.,
Radio Ministry of Northside Bible Church,
Wanneroo, Western Australia

"*Chasing Jesus* is the humorous, endearing, and soul-searching journey of a 'regular guy' finding the promise of Christian Joy that often seems elusive. This personal discovery is a practical account of what many believers and non-believers struggle with: *Where is God in my struggles?* Jack not only finds his Joy in God, but leaves a 'pebble-trail' that the rest of us can solidly walk to the feet of our Savior."

Nikki Nader, Lt. Col., USAF (ret.)

Earnest and entertaining…written with humility, humor and truly profound insights on nagging questions regarding "rubber meets the road" Christianity. A "tell it like it is", no holds barred personal conversation with the reader, based on this man's rich life adventure and searching. I know Christians of whatever persuasion will enjoy the journey. I sure did. His challenge to everyone, including himself, is summed up in the quote from St. Francis in the Closing Thoughts section of the book: "Preach the Gospel always. When necessary, use words".

Fr. Kevin Kirwan
Holy Annunciation Mission, Sioux City, Ia.
Author, *Finding Genuine Catholicism in the Orthodox East*

Jack's spiritual journey that is captured in Chasing Jesus was written as though he was witnessing my very journey through his eyes. From the first paragraph to the post-script, he engages the reader in a page-turning story as he navigates through his own quest in discovering Christianity. Jack leads the reader down a path of self-awareness that is guaranteed to stir a variety of emotions that at times brought me to tears. Chasing Jesus is unfiltered, visceral and heart-felt and is guaranteed to touch any individual, no matter where they are in their spiritual journey.

Mike Moravec
All Holy Spirit Greek Orthodox Church
Parish Council – Vice President
Omaha, Nebraska

5-STAR REVIEW...*CHASING JESUS* BY K. C. FINN FOR READERS' FAVORITE

Chasing Jesus is a short work of non-fiction on Christian themes of devotion and explorative Bible study, and was penned by author Jack Prohaska. Discussing a lifetime of experience, the nature of having faith in the difficulties of maintaining such faith in the modern world, this is a deeply personal journey made by the author and recounted in a conversational and often autobiographical style. Prohaska takes his readers along with him through a series of what he terms incredible "coincidences" that lead him through explorations of different belief systems, ultimately culminating in the Christ-risen Christianity which he now holds dear to his heart.

Though the narration is highly conversational and the plot lines of the biographical content sometimes take deviations here and there, what author Jack Prohaska has created is a lifetime in a book and a philosophy in which many readers with a crisis of faith are sure to find comfort. Christians, as the author rightly states, may have darker questions that they find difficult to voice, so having narration as astute and emotionally honest as Prohaska's really lends itself to the credibility of finding one's faith despite personal doubts and fears. I particularly enjoyed the wry humor and self-deprecating style of the author, whose down to earth dialogue is direct and engaging for readers to follow. Overall, *Chasing Jesus* feels like a life story told by one old friend to another, and as such, it delivers a powerful emotional authenticity alongside its hopeful and faithful devotion to God.

To Jesus…our Friend, Brother, and God.

TO MY READER: IMPORTANT...
"READ BEFORE READING!"

...Any similarity to a "normal" book is purely coincidental.

I'd like you to think of this effort of mine as a conversation between just you and me...one way, true, but a conversation nonetheless, and conversations have no outlines. They just flow, so the underlying themes tend to do their own dances in and out of the stream-of-consciousness narrative. I will be giving you my thoughts and can at least imagine what your responses to them might be (hopefully, positive).

These *essential* interactive themes are the insidious and dangerous Shallow-ization of Society, Heart-Wisdom, Holy Sorrow, and Joy (or "God-speak," as I've termed it). The single negative theme is the first, and it has a deleterious effect on the other three, which are related to each other in eminently positive ways.

The positive tradeoff in not having a "standard" presentation is, by definition, spontaneity—opportunities for changes of scenery along the way, little breaks in the action (*if* potentially entertaining and/or informative), a chance to insert humor or even pen a short poem (four in the book), give an interesting aside or quote consistent with the flow, occasionally revisiting something later with a comment or observation...

This book is then, in my thinking, "alive" in that it's kept its spontaneity and naturalness throughout—a joy to write, and I hope more entertaining to read *because* of its free-form style. The positive themes comprise a beautiful whole that I believe can bring us all closer to God. The sometimes-whimsical bits do not belie the depth and deadly seriousness of the essential message, the beating and bleeding heart of Holy Sorrow and its connection with Joy.

If you just go with the flow, I think we'll be okay.

I especially wanted this conversation with you to be free-wheeling and as entertaining as I could make it, consistent with the subject matter. Most importantly, I wanted it to be personal, intimate—just me (warts and all), you, my reader, and perhaps one more—our Lord, looking over our shoulders and blessing our hopeful efforts as we attempt to contemplate certain elements of the Faith with new, or at least unbiased and objective, eyes. Comments from my little focus group have ranged from, "Wow! I never thought of that!" to, "I figured I was the *only* one who thought that!"

Not far into the book lies the "jewel" of this effort, a legacy left us by C. S. Lewis, revealed there for any who are unaware of it. It holds profound potential for those open to it, no matter which faith community they may embrace.

But jewels require payment.

Christ brought glory through pain.

These, then, are the "lessons"—empathy and the wisdom of the heart.

If I could but lay my own heart open enough, and give wings to my tears, the stirrings of my soul might give me voice to adequately convey the beauty of that legacy. But I am only me—me, twenty-four hours a day, seven days a week—everybody else is taken, as I often say. I wrote *Chasing Jesus*. Should you ask, "Why?", I'd have to say, "There was nothing else for it."

So, my child takes flight, leaving the seminal nest with my hope that those stubby little wings will carry it to hearts and minds of you and others on this Christian path, *"Chasing" Jesus*.

We are all manuscripts in need of editing.

~jp

IN GRATITUDE

This effort started out as a lonely idea, spawned in an atmosphere in which under*whelming* would be an under*statement* regarding the enthusiasm of some whose early opinions and advice I sought. Certain friends and family, however, believed in me enough to not only offer encouragement, but also advice, healthy criticism, and even support, such as proofreading, and so on.

To these, I shall be forever grateful:

Grandson Corey and daughter Carol for advice, criticism, and/or support.

Grandson Shaun for early proofreading and suggestions.

Vince Russo, Lou Sinos, Jeff Johanesmeier, Vickie Hecker, Pete Wilger, Mike Moravec, and doctors Mark Purnell and Jeffrey Clark for taking the time to read the text and provide thoughtful and occasional technical criticism, as well as their warm encouragement.

Dr. Tom Walsh for his ever-loyal support and advice, as well as the correction of some silly mistakes and graciously providing the Foreword for the book.

My more than excellent editor, Rachel L. M. Hall for her invaluable work, going above and beyond my expectations.

My multi-talented son and partner in this effort, Brian, for taking the reins regarding everything from early proofreading and suggestions to handling so much of the "nitty-gritty" involved in getting the book published—as well as doing the artwork for the front and back covers as well as the marvelous illustrations throughout.

My oldest son, Mark, without whom this book would likely never have been written. He introduced me to C. S. Lewis, who in turn re-introduced me to Jesus.

My long-suffering wife, Diane, for not only having a hand in so many of the ancillary elements involved and offering sensible suggestions, but especially for her steadfast patience in putting up with the many idiosyncrasies and eccentricities of her euphemistically-termed "outside-the-box" husband all these years.

Finally, I really need to thank all my kids for just being who they are. Each, in his or her own special way, has been a source of inspiration. I've long felt that the lot of them are prob'ly better people than their old man.

~jp

FOREWORD

When I read Jack Prohaska's manuscript, my first thoughts were of an old song: "Love is where you find it, all around you, everywhere, in the air." When I substituted "God" for "love," I think I found the essence of what Jack was writing.

Then my next thought turned to one of my favorite Christian poets: Gerard Manley Hopkins. Consider the great verses from "As Kingfishers Catch Fire":

> I say more; the just man justices;
> Keeps grace, that keeps all his goings graces
> Acts in God's eye in what God's eye he is—
> Christ. For Christ plays in ten thousand places,
> Lovely in limbs, and lovely in eyes not His

These lines precede: "What I do is me, for that I come." Such exquisite words, so existentially precise, ring true to me all the days of my life. There is so much joy (C. S. Lewis' word, incidentally, for a profound and mysterious experience) in the heart-rending nature of Christian action that it must be pursued as often as possible, often without any tangible rewards. In these actions, as described in the book, Jack found his reason for being, providing what he calls his astounding epiphany.

An epiphany, with its lightning-strike effect, by its very nature, will not come often, but such moments are those we search for and try to recognize for what they mean in our lives. Early on, Jack provides the philosophical premises for his search: love, kindness, the many virtues tied to any happiness we can find. A quote from St. Francis in the book says, "Preach the Gospel always; when necessary, use words." Jack's mission for many years has been to entertain groups of elderly and ill patients in hospitals and nursing homes with his voice and keyboard, performing virtually every genre of music from the 19th-century "Gay 90s" to the present. Audiences are often in wheelchairs, mostly awake and appreciative, but sometimes somnolent. Regardless, Jack and his troupe of Christian volunteers, *The Love Squad*, will persevere and try—through humor, dialogues, and nostalgic reminiscences—to entertain and bring back a bit of their youth to those who are lonely, heart-broken, often in pain, and sometimes in despair.

He has done this for over thirty years, and out of these experiences and personal visits with patients, he has brought joy and sometimes relief to countless suffering men and women.

I have come late to these spiritual practices and witnessed what Jack has wrought. Whatever the reader's bliss may be, I hope you find some of the Joy that Jack has barely outlined.

It is in the action, itself, that one discovers Jesus in men's faces and souls.

Dr. Thomas P. Walsh
Professor Emeritus, English Dept., University of Nebraska
at Omaha

"…let him take up his cross and follow Me."

PREFACE:
JUST YOU AND ME...INVITE TO A TRIP

I'd like you to take a journey with me, a most peculiar and wonderful one, I think. There will be stops along the way, changes of scenery, so to speak. Marvelous and inexplicable occurrences, questions that many Christians might harbor quietly and secretly in their hearts will be brought out into the open, as well as some surprising gems of wisdom that I believe have a wondrous potential to bring you joy and peace of soul. Oh, those gems don't come from *my* old brain. I'm just the farmer who perhaps has an eye for what to harvest. The planting's been done by those wiser than me.

They won't be things you generally hear about in church, if at all. That, I think, is the beauty of such concepts as Heart-Wisdom, "God-speak", and the phenomenon of Joy, or what I call a "whiff of heaven." They will likely be quite fresh to you, realities that underlie, if you will, our Faith. Stuff of the Divinity perhaps at times alluded to, but seldom, if ever, fleshed out and given the treatment it deserves.

So, come with me…

"If I don't make it to heaven, I'll worship You from hell!"

I said that to God, and it's illustrative of the zeal I hope to maintain right up to the finish line, when my fondest hope is to finally get answers to all this mush in which we struggle.

I don't know what I'd say to anyone who might ask me to encapsulate this effort. There are so many "parts" to it. Much has happened to me that I can't really explain. I, myself, am a weird duck in a lot of ways, always kidding and joshing people, acting the wit (I'm at least *half*way there!)—the quintessential wag/smart-aleck, yet sometimes not so with it myself:

(Just outside the doors of a Nebraska high school, circa 1950)

Friend: "Hey Jack, ask me if I'm an orange."

Me: "Okay. Are you an orange?"

Friend: "Yes. Now ask me if I'm a banana."

Me: "Are you a banana?"

Friend: "No, idiot. I just told you! I'm an *orange!*"

(Sound of crickets as a bemused Jack stands there, staring blankly at the budding comic heading off to tell his homeroom pals)

So, sometimes the windshield, sometimes the bug. With all the jesting and kidding in which I've been both perp and victim, I often find in myself a deadly seriousness when considering matters such as faith.

Serious, yet…

Just as I think of beauty as not only a gift from God, but evidence as well of His very existence, so might well be humor. I know of nothing more appealing than Christians, indeed any folks, who can laugh with others and at themselves.

Consider the joyous, jovial Christian, one who takes oneself far less seriously than one's faith. I think this sort might well be more pleasing to our Lord than a dour perfectionist, however pious. Who would be more attractive, likely more effective in representing our Faith to non-Christians? I think humor is one of the things that help to fill up the God-shaped holes in our spirits and can brighten our lives in what seems an ever-darkening world.

Christianity equates to *light*, not darkness.

I often imagine Jesus perhaps jesting with the apostles in the seminal days of our faith, maybe around a campfire on some shore under the stars He created. A pleasing picture, no?

I, by the way, am also cursed with insatiable curiosity and will watch everything from the occasional more adult-oriented, social commentary-type episodes of *The Simpsons* to the most critically acclaimed *Masterpiece Theater* presentations on PBS, and I will read everything from the Sunday funnies to the classics. This book spans those same levels regarding style, language, and purpose, and goes from the occasionally whimsical to the deadly serious.

I would say this to any potential reader: The book, the whole potpourri of stuff that's in it, experiences—some quite remarkable—opinions, ruminations, my hopeful attempts at poetry—all honest and from the heart. I have no illusions as to finding any universal acceptance of the opinions. Actually, *suspicions* might be more accurate in some cases. Trust me, many of them may seem well outside the box. Only someone with a room-temperature IQ thinks everyone can be pleased. I think if the Lord, Himself, came walking across Lake

Michigan, somebody'd complain He didn't have a permit. And here *I* am, just a poor old duffer wallowing in the shallows…

So, poor me. I don't know the total depth and extent of what I have here. I do know parts of it are important, even essential. The seemingly endless coincidences; the nights of unbidden thoughts and inspirations invading my sleep; what has dogged my consciousness and stalked my reveries; the very crying out of my own heart, my gut, my instincts: all tell me there are things here that should, indeed, *must* be said and shared.

And thus, the journey I relate. The tortuous odyssey of an oft-confused, "re-constituted" Christian, asking nagging questions, yet relating experiences that seem to point inexorably to a Godhead that delights in teasing with glorious little glimpses and hints of what lies just beyond what our poor minds can apprehend—requiring, instead, the language, the lingo of the heart.

Chapter Three, "Prelude to My Epiphany," includes the true story of "Buddy." It somehow, I believe, reveals the heart, so to speak, of this effort, in that it speaks of pain and hints, for those who might see it, of the necessity of pain for heart-wisdom and Joy.[1] My fondest hope is that those who are open to it will have a marvelous experience similar to mine, but if all this book does is open the doors a bit for some to a fuller understanding of these three "essentials", and thereby bring them closer to a true connection with their Maker, it will have been worth the writing and worth the reading.

---

1   Capitalized to distinguish a spiritual phenomenon from ordinary "joy."

As I write this on a bleak day in April 2020, I have no clue as to the potential success of this effort. There seem to be as many books as there are readers in this world. I think it would be very sad should it just go nowhere. I have "forwarded" some profound wisdom gleaned from men like C. S. Lewis and Peter Kreeft, wisdom that can be of great benefit, I believe, for Christians of *all* stripes.

Knowledge seems to have taken over from wisdom as time has gone on. Now, information (true *and* false) has usurped knowledge, and we seem to be increasingly foundering in vast informational seas of no depth, devoid of substance, and, too often, truth.

We're not in Kansas anymore, Toto.

The shallow-ization of society is no help to Christianity.

It's been said that we will, not only as individuals but also as the human race, all one day stand before God.

The serious Christian might well wonder why so many of us, believers and otherwise, foolishly pursue the frivolous and leave wanting that which matters. So many blithely avoid dealing in mind and heart with what might happen should the Second Coming become a here-and-now reality and this circus come to a screeching halt…

A sound…a plea…a hope
to deliver one last vesper hymn as truth…
Too late.
Voices dying in the twilight.
One long, crying, plaintive note.
A symphony of souls strikes final chords
and it ends.
The heavens split.

And in that void between time and eternity, Man.

His bestowed sovereignty, his charge in ruins,

eyes forced to behold the foul detritus of his failure.

Treasures squandered as millions starved.

A bruised and bleeding planet, the haunted eyes of

the hurting

bear witness brooking no rationalization.

All excuses, halted mid-breath,

mere blackened ashes spilling soundless from quivering lips.

Useless.

Creature meets Creator—naked, unmasked now, ashamed.

Yet...

Some have lived for a promise...

Or will we even look up from our cell-phones?

Tick-tock.

No answers as to why the most deadly serious of questions is ignored. Whether the ultimate procrastination or a nonpareil case of mass denial, to serious Christians, the hordes of unbelievers can seem like lemmings racing for the cliff. Could there be a more apt metaphor for today than the story of the Ark? Warnings, storm clouds ignored, the saddest of consequences...

No answers, and if there is any wisdom from me in this book, I'm sure it's quite minuscule. I have found wisdom others have mined from life and have seen, through the grace of God, how so much of what they've passed on to us has dictated my own surprising experiences.

This book at base is an attempt to pass on what has *been* passed on to me and to others.

I'm offering you quite an eclectic meal here at *Chez Prohaska,* perhaps more mid-western smorgasbord than gourmet fare. The entrée is the necessity of pain, the wisdom of the heart, and a surprising personal revelation I believe is connected to the special phenomenon, Joy. There are side-dishes: "suspicions", no-frills apologetics, some remarkable experiences, even bits of poetry (as above), as well as food for thought you may or may not prefer to ingest. Throw these out with the trash if you disagree or are bored.

The cook tried.

He knows he's not a chef.

~Jack
April, 2020

CHAPTER ONE:
SEARCHING, AND HOW I ENVY PAUL

"We hold fast and wait,"
"God in Hiding"

Am I the only one?

Okay, I suppose I should explain the title to you before I go any further. It's not me pursuing a fleeing deity, yelling, "Stop!" Christ isn't running anywhere. Jesus is always waiting. I'm reminded of the oft-asked, "Have you found Jesus?" and, of course, the smart-aleck answer, "I didn't know He was lost!" (cue rim-shot, cymbal-hit). *Why does ridicule come so easily for the unbelieving?*

Anyway, I found Jesus, all right. Check that. I'm thinking, even as I write this, it might be more accurate to say He found me, and continues to do so in a way, as you'll see.

Chasing Jesus is really a sort of metaphor for my Christian experience since good old C. S. Lewis' words brought me back into the fold. I also admit to thinking it's a rather "catchy" title and might just lead folks to say, "What the heck is *that* about?"

What I've been "chasing" is a communication—a communion, if you will—a dialogue with Him, and of course that means with God. Madness? You think? God doesn't talk to *us*, right? "It's our job to talk to Him and wait for answers to our prayers," you may say. But what if we only need to have our antennae out, our hearts open, and we can "receive"?

Certainly, there is a veil between the ineffable spiritual realm and poor little us. The language God uses is not our language. Earnest seekers face a lonely and uncharted course, with no compass, no handy sextant for eternity. The word *empirical* comes to mind, and I think of Saul on the road to Damascus. I've long envied Saul/Paul, despite the painful martyrdom.

God lifted the veil and made one of His cosmic exceptions with Saul when He spoke in the language of His creature. On that old, dusty road, this great persecutor of Christians, gobsmacked by that disembodied voice of Jesus. Awesome, terrifying—but what a blessing! Through all of what was to come, the unbelievable tasks set before him, the trials, the martyrdom, he had the advantage of one thing: empirical evidence of not only the existence of God, but the truth of Jesus as well!

So, the one who spoke so eloquently about faith had, ironically, a leg up on the rest of us, in that the "evidence of things not seen" didn't even have to apply to him!

We, on the other hand, are forced to pull ourselves up by our own bootstraps regarding faith, and "Blessed are those who have not seen and yet believe."

What happened to me was as close to empirical as I can ever imagine. It certainly bolstered and continues to immeasurably bolster my faith.

Face it. We doggedly hold fast and wait. A promise made around 2,000 years ago, yet to be fulfilled. We are required to believe in a God we've never seen, Whose voice we've never heard—a "God in Hiding," as it were. A God Who, though He may answer prayers, certainly does so on His own terms and inscrutable schedule, in ways we may not even recognize and, incidentally, a God Who seems to have the annoying, even rather maddening habit of reserving the harder times for the best of us while He lets some of the worst just skate along, messing it all up for everybody else.

God in Hiding. Perfectly understandable, upon reflection. He simply didn't want to create automatons, and He's not some cosmic Geppetto merrily pulling strings from on high, controlling our clacking gyrations down here. I think He wants us to love Him, and *that* takes free will, the ultimate double-edged sword. You're free to do as you will, you're free to pay the consequences.

With Christianity itself, things got much more complicated for me.

After my re-conversion, I yet found myself full of questions and doubts. Why was everything so convoluted and confusing? From Jesus' simple message and ministry so long ago, it had all splintered into reportedly between *thirty-five and forty-thousand* separate denominations, ranging from snake-handling to massive musical productions—each group totally convinced that they are the "true" faith. If only one of these deviations from what had to be that *original* Church from way back then actually has the whole truth, by definition, all those other thousands must each be wrong, in part or in whole. How imaginative, how innovative is man, really, to take that basic, uncomplicated message and way of worship prescribed by the apostles and chop it all up into these thousands of variations!

"Truth."…If you were born in Ireland, you're probably a Catholic. Sweden: a Lutheran; from Mississippi: likely Southern Baptist. And, by the way, Middle East: Muslim; China: Taoist or Confucianist; India: Hindu—on and on.

I found my church experience even more troubling and confusing. I'd finally discovered a church I believed (and believe) to be unchanged from the original, but shouldn't communication, communion with the Creator of All That Is be a joyous, visceral experience, something that shakes your very soul and leaves you in absolute awe? Maybe my fellow worshipers were feeling something like that, but they sure didn't look like it. It looked so much like just going through the motions. Where was the joy, the excitement—yes, even the tears one might expect?

I would pray on the way to church to be let into that "circle of grace," as I saw it, to be able to *feel* this ineffable, unwordable Majesty. I recited prayer and creed with as much sincerity and intensity as I could possibly muster. There had to be more, somehow. I often thought of that old Peggy Lee song, "Is That All There Is?"

The practices of my particular church are, after all, holy mysteries, far beyond my poor capacity to begin to understand, but wouldn't God want me to truly experience Him, to know, deep within my soul, that He was, as in the prayer, "Burying Himself in me, that I might bury myself in Him"? Was there somehow something else, some additional path, if you will, to that for which I so longed?

At this time, I could never have imagined what was going to come out of left field and make so many questions nearly moot. It was all *who?*, *what?*, and *why?*. And, *Am I the only one who has this longing? Am I the odd-man-out, or are a good number of my brethren in the same boat, but nobody's saying anything? If so, are those of us with this problem somehow inadequate? If only some "insiders" are able to "get it," then why? And what can I do to join THAT group?*

I decided to boil Christianity down to its basic element, namely Christ. What I wanted, at base, was simple—to somehow *experience* Christ, to feel Him on that visceral level my heart and soul demanded.

But at this point, it was just a bunch of questions. I wanted to look with a totally unbiased eye at things, if that's ever truly possible. Maybe I could un-muddy the waters. Maybe I could list and look at questions I'd never heard addressed in sermons—questions I've had and have heard others ask only in private, perhaps for fear of being somehow outside the norm. (Can you say *heretic*?) I could perhaps bundle them all up, put them in the other room and zero in my mind on Jesus alone. I wanted to take a mental/spiritual shower and stand unclothed before my Lord. I was seeking an addition *to*, not a substitute *for* my Christian worship/experience.

The next chapter, *Questions and Suspicions,* is not "required reading," but I've begun to realize the portion on the heart is a virtually essential prelude to what I think of as the "meat" of this effort, which you'll discover in Chapter Six, *"Epiphany! …The Surprise and the Connection"*. I could just meet you there, but I really think you should stay with me here. It's a crazy world out there at best, and "best" you and I take a good look at it. After all, *"Whom the gods would destroy they first make mad"* (ancient pagan proverb).

There may be some questions *you've* had. If I sound too sure of anything, truly, I'm not. I might get caught up a bit in the writing, but as I said earlier, some of what I'm bringing up, particularly regarding the Old Testament, involves what are actually nagging suspicions regarding the spiritual slalom course I've been negotiating…

CHAPTER TWO:
QUESTIONS AND SUSPICIONS

"God no oxymoron," "Why them, not me?", and "Wisdom of the Heart"

"The heart is known as the seat of knowledge."

~From the Ascetic Writings of the Church

No need to leave the house to see the circus.

Think on this: can our lives on this earth be called anything but insane? Put aside the madness of ISIS, broken governments infested with corruption or, at minimum, trapped in calcified impotence—right here, in our own society, don't you sometimes sense things are off-kilter? No need to leave the house anymore to go to the circus. The news channels give us Washington, a host of balancing acts and no shortage of clowns. Men are rewarded with multiple millions for carrying an inflated leather ball over some white lines or stuffing one through a hoop, while educators who help shape our youth—by definition, the future of our society/civilization, are paid a pittance by comparison. Rock stars and actors are idolized, nearly deified, and made obscenely rich, while *true* heroes are yesterday's news before sundown.

Can anyone find sanity in the fact that a boxer now has a third of a *billion-dollar* contract to pound away on others in a roped-off square while masses flee his country to escape poverty?

I know: "free market," "what it'll bear," and so on. But what of our priorities? Isn't something fouled up here, really? If so, what? Can we pin it down—expose it?

Potter Stewart, a former Supreme Court Justice, unable to define pornography, ended his statement with "but I know it when I see it."

One might suspect a basic flaw in man, this "Coliseum" syndrome, the misplaced idolatry—just another result of the Fall, among many.

"...sound and fury, signifying nothing."

~*Shakespeare*

Shakespeare...mankind, metaphorical stage, fictional plotline. Aren't we primarily unwitting characters in a grand fiction made up of wishful thinking and denial? Isn't it a fiction that all the material things being foisted on us from every quarter are going to bring actual happiness? The social media explosion: Surely it's good to share beautiful experiences and uplifting thoughts with friends and family, but is anyone out there really waiting with bated breath for the earth-shattering update on what I had for dinner last night or the new shirt I just bought? We're drowning in a deluge of online selfies. I thought the Me Generation was over, but it looks like the Selfie Generation is the latest iteration—it just has a new name and time.

I heard the term *infantilizing* the other day. Are we, with some of our magnificent technologies, encouraging infantile levels of thought in the long run—are we creating some sort of organic robots, pathologically dependent on tiny communication devices?

To step back and really, *really* take a clear look at this world in which we struggle—to honestly consider not only our lives in general, but all the confusion regarding faith, in particular…it could well inspire the writing of an intro for the old *Twilight Zone* series.

I think I will.

(Imagine the voice of Rod Serling)

Consider, if you will, Halloween night in Everytown— giggling goblins out looking for porchlights and plunder. No one expects any more distortion of reality than the fun house mirror down at the county fair. But if you look carefully, you might just see something slithering out of the inky shadows. It wears a shifting mask as old as time itself—and it's not looking for candy…

So, we have a ghoul with myriad names, hiding behind ever-changing masks. Some we can recognize: confusion, obfuscation, misdirection—the usual smoke and mirrors of the disingenuous.

More insidious and deadly sobriquets are far less obvious: frivolous pursuits, shallow thinking—all that consumes not only our treasure but our time and our minds.

We arrive "home" at last, at life's end, with a sack full of nothing.

But I digress.

Agnostics have a bit of a bad rap among believers. Their stance is simply that nothing can be known beyond the material, and at first blush, one can detect some logic, in that what we allow into our consciousness, with regard to intellectual, abstract information, is invariably hearsay. Someone said it, someone wrote it. Whatever truth or untruth is conveyed comes through the filter of man, the same creature who found ways to split Christianity into those myriad shapes and sizes, historically finding excuses to hate, and even destroy non-believers as well as fellow Christians who might dare to disagree.

Looks like most of temporal life is really just a big *maybe*, with plenty of *so whats* thrown in—even in Christianity as a whole, with all its competing variations, confusion, and often apathy on many levels. So many minds are closed off to any questions whatsoever…

As is said: "Through a glass, darkly." Yes, or one might indeed liken the entire physical realm to a fun house mirror when comparing it to the true reality on the other side of that veil. Real, but distorted, somehow. Herculean efforts by philosophers, psychologists, and thinkers of all stripes to make sense of all this mush end up as just more mush. No more agreement in the political and social arenas than in the religious, with its thousands of strains and brands.

Question: Have you ever wondered why certain sections of the Old Testament seem to be rare (if not totally absent) in sermons, and so on? I have a suspicion. Were I priest or preacher, I imagine I'd have a tough time talking about how the magicians in Egypt changed all the rivers to blood, as an example.

I'm reminded of the title of Judge Judy's book: *Don't Pee on My Leg and Tell Me It's Raining!*

'Nuff said.

The Old Testament is rife with simply incredible stuff. Okay, the fallback position of an Old Testament apologist might be, "Well, with God, all things are possible—He was just using those ancient magicians for some mysterious purpose of His own." All right, I'll concede we can leave it at that. But what about all the *God-ordered* genocide— whole populations cruelly destroyed, men, women, innocent children. Captives taken, forced into slavery? I'm not even detailing the more gruesome Nazi/ISIS-worthy stuff.

Have you not found the contrast between the two testaments both stark and shocking? Blood spilled in vengeance vs. blood spilled in love, darkness vs. light, and a God we struggle to make sense of, Who, on that night in Bethlehem, seems to change in the blink of an eye...

A syllogism:

> *IF...*
> A) We accept it as true that God is a loving God,
> *AND...*
> B) The Old Testament paints Him as some kind of
> cruel monster,
> *THEN...*
> C) The Old Testament would *seem* to be wrong (in *this*
> regard).

Isn't it this sort of thing that gives atheists so much ammunition? Personally, no matter how hard I try, I can't see God as an oxymoron, a "loving monster." I am no biblical scholar, but I don't believe I checked my brains at the door when I returned to Christianity. I take heart that I've even heard Orthodox priests admit (though somewhat grudgingly, I felt), that the Old Testament has a good deal of hyperbole, metaphor, allegory (emphasis on the *gory*), even myth. Why? I suspect one would have to understand ancient mindsets, superstitions, and so on. Work for scholars, and miles above *my* pay grade. (I must add that there are great truths in many myths, some that can only be conveyed in story-form, etc.)

But the question follows as relentlessly as those plagues in the narrative: if some of the Old Testament is somehow not factual, where can the *line* be drawn? Is this why an ultra-devout and learned Christian I know refuses to even read the Old Testament? (This was likely at the advice of his spiritual advisor who, I'm sure, advises many, so he's probably not alone in this.) Is it that those with this attitude toward the O. T. just can't decide which parts to accept as literal?

When I asked a priest about some confusion I had about the creation story, I was told that before Adam and the Fall, there was no death. The "lion was lying down with the lamb" right from the start. Apparently, the dinosaurs didn't get the message and were blithely chomping away on each other all those millions of years. The only way out of this enigma is if man is created *before* T. Rex and friends, so Eve and hubby will be there to *cause* the Fall and the chaos! (Just saying…)

To me, it's the ultimate conundrum. The Bible is the inspired word of God, yet apparently one would have to assume the equivalent of white being black to be able to accept every single word of the Old Testament as being literally true. There are answers to this, and I have faith He will answer them for me on the other side if I don't get them here. As a Christian, I have no intention of taking even one word away from the O. T. We are warned against that. As a Christian, I also believe honest questioning is far better than blind obedience without using the brains God gave us. I can only be honest with myself and others, pray over this, and keep querying those who might have answers.

One question from my early church experience was this: How can there even *be* unfriendly Christians? A contradiction in terms, right? Mustn't judge, even though I'd seen so many seemingly unfriendly, unwelcoming folks in church. That struck me as a strange way to be "making disciples of all nations"! Then I considered the fact that we "judge" all the time. Crossing the street, we judge how safe it'll be. We judge which church to attend, which foods to eat, and so on, and so on…

How about *discerning*? How about simply using our gray matter to evaluate and make decisions? How about judging, in the biblical sense, being something more like *condemning* (which falls under God's purview)? In the first hot flush of my re-born, and now serious, Christianity, I naively imagined joining all these soul-mates, this band of brothers and sisters on fire for the Lord. A golden community of the saved, joyous in their prayers and worship, venturing out into the world—visiting the elderly and infirm, by their example attracting all those fallen souls out there...

Early on I joined a church where nearly all of the congregation appeared quite emotionless, many of them seeming almost cold. (Talk about church lacking the "Wow" factor!) They couldn't *all* be ill or depressed. Something had to be missing here. I thought again of the Supreme Court Justice— "but I know it when I see it." I realized I wasn't to judge individuals, but I couldn't avoid looking at the whole picture and discerning something wrong—out of frame or focus, if you will. If it walks like a duck and quacks like a duck, it's probably Donald or Daffy—but who am *I* to say?

So what, anyway? We know we're never perfect. The Church has been described as a hospital for sick souls. Aren't we all spiritually ill in so many ways? Aren't we each to "remove the log from our own eye"? Don't we all need to clean up our own houses? Yes, yes, and yes. But the question wouldn't go away. Where was the *fire*? Emily Dickinson would likely describe the various elements of worship as the "essence" of Christian practice, but ask, "Where is the *phosphorescence?*" Why couldn't I see something happening around me, feel something within me rattling down to the roots of my soul? God is Ultimate Majesty—awesome, terrifying presence and love beyond measure. All those around me must have been feeling, experiencing something profound or they wouldn't keep coming back, week after week. Right?

An intriguing question—a what-if: What *if* this very non-experience of profound feelings was actually an element of faith—not only the evidence of things not seen, but also of things not *felt*?

So, I might have been the only one who didn't somehow get it, or I might not be alone. Did God want us to have our souls stirred by these practices or was He testing the faith of some, or all of us, by *not* allowing feedback, so to speak? All I could do was continue praying for enlightenment. I couldn't escape this aching desire to feel Him on a gut-level, and in fact, I couldn't avoid the thought that that's what all the dynamics of the Faith are about. Liturgies, prayers, Holy Communion—all to *interact*, if you will, with the Master, the Author of Life. To commune in the deepest sense, at least for me, seemed to require something in addition to what I was doing/experiencing. Was there something...

Anything?

You know, God's given us eyes with which to see, ears to hear, but don't we *know* some things that go beyond our physical senses? What makes you somehow know that brutality towards children and animals, for instance, is wrong? Your eyes see it, your ears hear it, but that stirring inside your soul, that sickening feeling, the disgust—ah, that's something else, isn't it? We know with the *heart*.

"Know with the heart." No brain cells in the heart. What is it about the heart? It's not a sensory organ as such. We hear with the ear, that other conduit joining the eye for intellectual input. We feel with fingers, smell with noses, taste with tongues—but what is this with the heart? Are we referring to a physical organ when we say things like "He has a broken heart," " Her heart's not in it," or when we utter a "heartfelt prayer"? We say, "He's got heart." What was the song "Your Cheatin' Heart" referring to? Isn't this heart often paradoxically the cause of its own heartbreak? Doesn't it often foolishly lead us astray? What is it, where is it, why is it?

It seems we have a sort of spiritual/emotional "twin," or counterpart, to the physical organ that pumps our life's blood. They even act like twins. Often, when one's heart is broken, an aching pain is reported in the physical heart. Sadly, no EKGs, no stress-tests for a phantom organ—only our haunting suspicion of an ethereal *something*...

But allowing for imperfections—the eyes, ears, and so on can often deceive us as well—the heart seems to allow us to soar to places the mind cannot reach. Since the spiritual realm is not *our* playground, we can hardly expect our normal senses, even our intellects, to tell us a whole lot about it. Indulge me here: what if the language of God is the language of this mysterious spiritual organ we all refer to but can't really describe? (Much like God Himself, now that I think about it.)

What *if* He left His "fingerprints" in some way when He authored our existence? What if He embedded within us with something that might allow us to see glimpses of Him? What would these be like, and how would we recognize them? Would we have any means of accessing them?

God in Hiding might just be playing hide and seek with us.

Or was I just nuts? Was I whistling in the dark, dreaming up something that isn't there at all? Was I simply grasping for some sort of crutch or excuse for whatever I seemed to lack in my spiritual experience proper?

I spoke earlier of the fun house mirror effect, the distortion of reality. A fogged-over fun house, and we're stuck in it. Yet—what might be filtering through that veil separating us from the spiritual realm? Even a distorted mirror reflects much of reality.

In my own unabashed fit of metaphor fever, I once described our temporal lives as "Riding the Funnyville Trolley all the way down to Grab-Your-Anklesburg." (Confession is good for the soul.)

Either way, I had to think that whatever communication from on high (if indeed it is being sent) must reach us here in the gross material realm via this spiritual heart. We certainly weren't getting anything of this sort through our physical senses. I am not implying that Holy Communion isn't a spiritual/physical communication, and God certainly leaves clues in abundance in all the beauties of nature for us to see, hear, smell, and so on, but I'm speaking of something quite different here.

Perhaps it's something that would come from inside us. If it were a sentence, an object without subject or verb—something just *there*. Much like a chip we implant in a beloved pet, could it allow us to come home in some spiritual sense? Is there a message for the heart in a broken, nearly-deaf world where for the first time in history (as far as I know) unabashed evil has come out of the shadows and is brazenly giving a middle-digit salute to civilized society?

On this inane and insane planet, where fools make fools of the wise and even men of goodwill cannot agree on much of anything, even truth itself seems at times a shape-shifting phantom. What message might be filtering through that veil that separates us from ultimate truth and sanity? Is our Father whispering hope, "soft as the voice of an angel," as in that old song?

Can we hear it?

CHAPTER THREE:
PRELUDE TO MY EPIPHANY

*...groundwork for a surprising
and profound phenomenon*

"Joy is the serious business of Heaven."

~*C. S. Lewis*

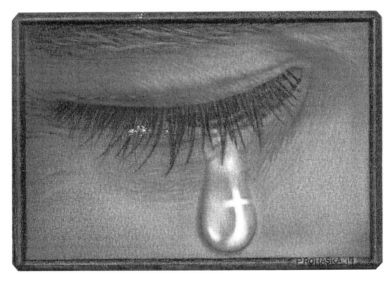

Let your heart freely bleed for these...

Where to begin? Sadly, yet interestingly, I think it begins with pain, the blood brother of empathy.

I'm speaking here of that faithful companion of true compassion, Holy Sorrow. Mother Teresa was an expert on this kind of pain, suffering her "dark night of the soul" after witnessing unending poverty and suffering over so many years. One imagines nightmares—hungry, haunted eyes, the whole tragic morass of misery in which she endlessly soldiered on—waking realizations that it was like trying to empty the ocean with a teaspoon...

Let me guess your question.

You must be thinking, *Why is he talking about pain? What's that about? What can this possibly have to do with the "medium" he mentioned at the get-go?*

Everything.

The yin and yang of the heart. I posit that the heart must be vulnerable to breakage, even willingly broken, to truly love. If you can't hurt, you can't love—not only man-woman love. I believe the pain of this hurting world must be taken in, digested, and metamorphized into tears for the suffering. I imagine a weeping Savior with outstretched hand, whispering to those with ears to hear, "Join me. Take up my cross. Let your heart freely bleed for the agonies of all these others."

This, then, must be the territory of Joy.

(No, that's not a misprint.)

Coincidentally, as I sat down to write just now, I took a detour to my e-mails and opened one with horrific pictures and the story of a terribly abused baby pitbull. My own puny, ever-insufficient efforts for children and animals are tiny microcosms of the real work of Mother Teresa and the even broader efforts of whole groups of saintly folks all over the globe, but my tears at this very moment remind me to tell you that sorrow and pain don't lead to, or call up this special Joy but are necessary for it—creating fertile ground in the heart.

You'll note I said Joy—not to be confused with normal happiness, or even pleasure—our usual desire-fulfillment patterns. Not simply a "Hoop-de-doo, fiddle-dee-dee, let's party" kind of joy, as you will see. It's also something I don't think you would trade for anything in this world, if and when you experience and recognize it.

Interested? Then I should get to my story. As I hinted, before so rudely interrupting myself, I think my own path to the answer to my worship dilemma began with pain.

Certainly, there is pain in witnessing the cosmic sea-change around us—evil gleefully flaunting its dirty laundry in our faces, while good men and whole nations seem paralyzed, frozen in some inexplicable apathy—millions disenfranchised, starving, brutalized… smaller, more personal pain can hit just as hard and mean as much.

"Buddy."

I had been visiting folks in nursing homes for quite some time when I found "Buddy." I'd always tried to find a lonely someone who "had no one". The activities staff member suggested Buddy, saying only that he was paralyzed. For some reason, she added, "But he seems aware…"

Buddy was totally paralyzed from the neck down. He was unable to speak—head and eye movement only.

I stepped into his little room, introduced myself, and pulled up a chair beside his bed, pasting what I hoped was a cheerful-looking smile on my face, all the time thinking, *Lord! What must this be like? What kind of horror is this? Lying there 24/7, day after day, month after month. Year after year? Thank the Lord for TV!*

I went home that afternoon and tried to "be" Buddy—to experience what it must be like. Disciplining myself as I lay on my bed, moving my eyes and head only, I looked at the ceiling, started imagining shapes in the shadows of the room…I lasted about an hour before beginning to appreciate the horror. The thought of even twenty-four hours of this was almost beyond imagining. Years of this? Oh, my.

But what could *I* do? What could I offer this poor wretch? How could I even be sure he understood what I was saying? What might mean something to him, add something to his day to alleviate, for whatever little bit of time, this unending, stupifying boredom?

So much better if he were just dead.

As a Christian, this unwelcome, shocking thought appalled me. Purely pragmatically, it made sense, particularly should Buddy be a right-with-God Christian. *A blessing then*, I had to think, *of the first order.*

It's often said, "Do something good for someone, and you'll feel the better for it." Not so. Not for me. At least, not in this case.

Buddy was in hell. I could only see it that way. My own little hell was walking in every week with that stupid grin on my face, trying to make "bricks without straw". I had no instruction book for this sort of thing, so I was playing it by ear—the game: no real rules, no clear payoff at the end…

How long might I do something without ever knowing I did something?

Who did I think I was?

Who did Buddy think I was?

Did Buddy even think?

In a way, I hoped he didn't. That way, the endless, stultifying ennui would just be a slow march of nothingness—Buddy at peace.

Me off the hook.

I think part of me knew even then that something was happening here. I couldn't go home with my tail between my legs and just call it a bad job, no matter how tempting. But without feedback? All my efforts might just mean zip, nada. Wouldn't it be better to go somewhere else where I could at least see *results*, good or bad?

Or—was there some way I could gauge a response?

Perhaps...

the eyes.

The scene:

I enter the room as usual. It's been a couple of weeks since this started. I'd hooked up a spare VCR unit I had to his TV, and I'm bringing in the first of the comedy tapes I've planned on using. Fingers crossed, I ask the nurse to prop his head forward and raise that part of the bed so he can see comfortably. A silent prayer, and we begin.

At first, nothing. About three minutes in, I think I see a flicker in his eyes. Imagination? Wishful thinking? A few minutes later, his head bends back and his mouth opens in what looks like a yawn, but with a sound—a sort of "braying"...

It had followed right on the heels of a punchline!

Slowly, his eyes leave the TV, and after a bit, he's looking right at me. That moment—well, as they say about Zen and has been said of special Joy, "If you can say it, it isn't it."

That moment, frozen in time and memory—he, from his silent and solitary confinement, me from my busy, harried world, reaching for each other wordlessly, without sound or gesture.

Only eyes.

What has happened, my friend? Did you enjoy that? What lies behind those eyes? My mind reaches across the silent abyss…

Silence never so profound, nor any room so distant from the world outside. There *was* no world outside at this moment.

Only eyes.

And it seems nothing has ever felt so good, so right.

End of scene.

But we're in the fun house after all, and perfection is reserved for heaven. Buddy's story is here on earth in a dingy little room over-looking a parking lot. His story, our interaction is, as is everything else in life, a mixture. The comedy tapes worked beautifully for a long time, but the day came when he slowly turned his head away. Of course, I didn't understand. What was the problem? I tried different types of humor—bringing in sitcoms, subtler standups, less subtle standups, monologues…

Nothing.

When you've been to the mountaintop, the valley can seem so low. It seemed I'd lost him somehow. Earlier, I spoke of the heart being broken. Maybe it's more like being melted. Melted down into something warmer, more pliable, malleable—attracting pain into one chamber, expelling empathy and compassion out the other. (As to *my* strange journey, I only know as time goes on, I realize I am increasingly becoming a crybaby of sorts, ever more affected by things.)

In Buddy's case, it was just confusion and frustration.

I would try a new tack. Maybe, just maybe—we could somehow communicate. But I needed a medium. A medium and a method.

The eyes.

Like some frenzied Tom Swift, I began to make a chart. The alphabet, of course, and a list of the most used words in the English language, and some of the most commonly used phrases tailored, as much as I could, to Buddy's situation. My plan was simple, and I thought myself a genius. He could blink once for *yes*, twice for *no*, as I would merrily point to letters, words, phrases to allow him to answer any questions I had. I would ask if *he* had questions, uncovering his heart and feelings as if I was at Bletchley Park in World War II, solving the Enigma Code. *Down with Doenitz and his bloody U-boats!*

You may have already guessed it.

I'm not sure, but I think it was even raining that day, a sodden and dreary backdrop to my disappointment. The greater frustration was not that it didn't work. By now, I'd come to understand some facial expressions, and he just didn't seem interested. Once more, confusion. I cursed the fact that I couldn't just ask him what he wanted.

Buddy just lay there.

But I couldn't walk away—not yet. Whether he liked it or not, I was going to do something for him.

Then I thought of a prayer.

There is a special prayer, well-known I believe, in most liturgical churches, called *The Jesus Prayer*. It says, "Lord Jesus Christ, Son of God, have mercy on me, a sinner." The prayer is repeated over and over until it hopefully becomes absorbed into one's heart.

I decided to offer it to Buddy as a sort of "mantra", something he could focus his mind on constantly. It was as much a mind-control thing as a spiritual exercise—a "win-win" that just might replace that horrific boredom, however temporarily.

Last hope.

I shortened the prayer to (inhale) "Lord Jesus Christ," (exhale) "have mercy on me," and told him to concentrate on this prayer, to let it become a part of him, to "become" the prayer, so to speak. And, of course, I prayed.

Hard.

I held little hope of success a week later as I rather reluctantly crossed the threshold of that little room. Silly notion, after all. What was I thinking? I didn't even know if Buddy was a Christian!

Well, "In for a penny…"

Into his room I went—stupid grin, pull up the chair. Looking down at him like a schoolteacher querying a kid on his homework, I asked a question that could have no answer but silence. I felt I must be mad.

"Buddy, you try the prayer I gave you?"

Can a shock occur gradually?

It began at the corners of his mouth.

Slowly, like shadows fleeing a sunrise, it spread and brightened— some muscles, likely long-dormant, began to stretch. His eyes riveted me. I've heard of smiles that can light up a room, but this one lit up my soul. I didn't know he even *could* smile! For one golden moment in my life, I knew I'd brought a bit of relief into someone's hell. Something had worked.

Praise God!

But…

Mountains and valleys. Here in our fun house, change seems the sole constant. A punch in the gut, a heart-wrench awaited me. It would be my first conscious understanding of heart-pain, as well as that which would become the heart, so to speak, of this book.

Shortly after that miraculous smile, Buddy's inexplicable lack of interest seemed to begin again. Over the weeks that followed, though I believed he must be benefitting from the prayer, he just appeared to be losing interest in anything beyond what might be in his own sealed mind. He could be at peace. Hopefully, he had what he needed and I was now superfluous.

He might also be losing all cognition.

Funny world. Unhealthy food and vices always seem to taste best and tempt the most. Whole-wheat bread can taste like cardboard; moral virtues and healthy exercise demand sacrifice and effort. The beauty and brutality of nature: how majestic the lion downing its prey; how awesome and mind-boggling the tornado, the lightning storm.

You want perfection?

You might as well try to grasp water in your fist.

Finally, the day came when Buddy turned his head away as I walked into the room.

I gave up. Not that day. It was gradual. Weekly visits turned into monthly, then every other month. Finally, I shelved Buddy. I had done what I could, I was sure.

I saw him one last time at a musical performance I gave at his nursing home. He was wheeled in and his wheelchair placed in the front row. He looked exactly as I last saw him.

The eyes.

They gazed fixedly at me throughout the performance, no expression on that frozen face. I was somehow unnerved. *Why do I feel pangs of—what? Guilt? Are those eyes accusing me?*

It was over. The room was cleared, except for Buddy and a few other wheelchair-bound residents. I (rather hurriedly) packed up my equipment and prepared to leave. I stopped by his chair.

What did I say to him? I honestly don't remember.

One thing I do recall, and often wish I didn't...

Tears.

Oh, Buddy... What do those tears mean? If only I had the wisdom. My heart is so broken for you. I could not reach into your hell enough to understand, and I don't know even now that I didn't let you down. Did I? Then why couldn't God have told me what to do? We did a strange dance, you and I. I had to lead. Did I somehow stumble and fail you?

My hell is that this side of that veil, I'll never know.

Buddy's story ends here. A short time later, I inquired about him. They can't tell non-family outright anymore, but I know the code.

He'd passed.

My prayer, should I make it past the Golden Gates someday, is to run into Buddy. I imagine he'll talk my leg off.

It's my turn to listen.

CHAPTER FOUR:
JOY

*A "whiff of heaven" and two ultimately
indescribable 3-letter words*

"God's affectionate whisperings—benign and pleasant hauntings"

~Me

"Our best havings are wantings."

~C. S. Lewis

I started blubbering like a baby.

As I mentioned about Zen, if you can say it, it's not it. You can only get at it in any measure by saying what it *isn't*—much as a sculptor chips away at raw stone to get down to and reveal the work of art already in the rock. As to this particular Joy to which I refer, actually, much can be said around it, if you will. That to which it points, however, is a different story. We can only comprehend the workings, the energies of it, not its essence, for it points ultimately to God.

My first hint of something "East and West of the world" (Lewis, again) came on another visit to a nursing home a few years after Buddy. Things hadn't changed much. I was still looking for a lonely soul who might appreciate a visitor. Again, they gave me someone who had lost the ability to speak. She communicated by typing with one finger, slowly, on a gadget similar to a tablet…

Problem was, it kept going south on her. We had to restart it with a bent paperclip pushed into a tiny hole in the back and wiggled until the unit came alive again. It was a terribly arduous and frustrating way to communicate with each other. Hours crawled by…

Finally, I came to understand that she was desperate for spiritual support and prayer. Apparently, what little money she had she was sending off every month to some avaricious TV evangelists! I knew the reputations of some of them, and I was appalled. Here was this elderly invalid, living in her tiny room with almost no possessions, being taken by a bunch of shameless charlatans. I promised I'd get a *real* Christian clergyman up to see her as soon as possible.

Again…

The eyes.

Silently bearing witness to understanding and joyous anticipation.

This time, I knew what the tears meant.

I'm pressing the *pause* button on my story for a bit because I'll be sailing into uncharted seas soon, and before I try to navigate those waters, I feel I should tell you some things. I say *uncharted* because I'll soon be telling you about something unsought, unimagined, entirely unexpected that occurred and continues to occur—something I have never heard of, never read about, never dreamed of…

I am on my own lonely island in this, not knowing if my experience is unique to me. It seems highly unlikely, as I believe its "engine" is available to anyone, save perhaps the most hateful, bitter, unfeeling among us. I also don't know its actual relationship to Joy, beyond my heart seeming to tell me so emphatically that the phenomena are at least related, if not one and the same.

What I do know is—and I can tell you this, my dear reader, with all my heart—it happened and continues to happen. It is deep, it is profound, and it is beautiful, and I truly wouldn't trade it for anything in this world.

In the final analysis, if anyone out there finds it happening to him or her, this effort will be worth it (emphasis on *happening)*. It will come unbidden, from out of the blue. Again in the words of the Justice: you'll know it when you see it. At the very least, some may recognize Joy for the first time, realize its source, and know that source can feed their soul. That alone would be a true blessing!

But, as with Buddy, I'll never know the ultimate results of this hopeful endeavor in my earthly life.

Now, on with my story.

First Inklings

Exhausted from hours of dogged, frustrating effort (and with my blood pressure likely doing its own dance), I headed for the elevator. Weary satisfaction would best describe my mood—grateful that something good had come of it all, but completely drained. Just as the doors opened, it happened. I started blubbering like a baby! Great sobs poured out of me, and my heart felt like it would burst. Embarrassment vied with shock and surprise as my primary reaction.

But was there something else, as well?

Initially, I thought, as I imagine *you* must be thinking, *Overly-tired, relieved to be out of there…perfectly natural reaction.*

But there was a *hint* of something just out of reach. It somehow went beyond the poignancy of the combination of sadness for the condition of a helpless, naïve old woman and the great satisfaction that something went right. I didn't know then, couldn't imagine, that those two might be inseparable.

Christ brought glory through pain.

As the elevator descended, I returned to "normal" and headed for my next appointment, a meeting with my new church's men's group. I put it all down to being a nice, satisfying experience, no more, no less.

Halfway through the meeting, it happened again. I was relating the details of my visit, and I broke down completely. Not only that, it happened once more when I was telling my good wife about it, hours later. What was going on? I'd never been like this before.

In the days that followed, I gradually put the whole thing on the back burners of my mind. Time has its way of mellowing or actually deadening memories of even the most gripping experiences, and so I rumbled on with my life, barely giving the "elevator incident" a thought. Sure, it seemed profound at the time, but after all, I was mentally and psychically bone-weary. That, mixed with the deep satisfaction that I'd delivered a blow to the bad guys—one less fish for their insatiable nets—must have created an emotional overload. I was simply reacting to it.

But even as I tried to satisfy myself with these reasonings, there lurked a nagging suspicion of something undefinable, something just beyond my consciousness, that had accompanied the opening of those elevator doors.

At this point, my story starts to get legs. A seemingly serendipitous series of events will lead inexorably to what I've discovered about my heart and myself, Joy, and "whisperings of the Master."

Side-note here. Should you be wondering at this point if I might have been fooling myself and shoehorning things into my experience that I wished to occur, I will give you four "*un*-s": they were all *un*sought for, *un*prayed for, *un*expected, and *un*imagined. (Incidentally, my prayer life has been much the same. So much of what I pray for doesn't happen, though I often get something far better. In fact, most of the really important things in my life have been things for which I *haven't* prayed, but for which I'm eternally grateful.)

It has been a fascinating ride. I hope you'll find it so as well.

CHAPTER FIVE:
THE REST OF THE STORY

...an invasion of coincidences driving me to where?

"The winter night offers its pure cup to heaven...Will He Who made our eyes not see me?"

~*Émile Verhaeren*

Blood Shed   In the blink of an eye?   Blood Given

Unbidden. It's all been unbidden. (Another *un-*.) My very return to Christ was an inexplicable series of improbable happenings. I'll not take the time to bore you with them. I'll only say they finally culminated in a few short sentences in C. S. Lewis' signature work, *Mere Christianity*, a book suggested by my firstborn son, who'd been doggedly praying for me since dirt. An intellectual hurdle was finally cleared and a strange and wonderful journey began.

The first of these occurrences was my stumbling across a CD that seemed to describe something called JOY.

As I hadn't had much of *that* since becoming a Christian, and as you've seen, was quite confused about the whole business, I thought, *What the heck, if I can actually get some pleasure and satisfaction out of my Christianity, it's gotta be worth a listen.*

There were strange but interesting references to a different way of "hearing about" or "hearing" God.

What? What's that got to do with enjoyment? Really? Come on! I've got the Bible to tell me about God. There must be 10,000-plus books on the subject. How many sermons have I heard about God—a hundred? More? The scriptures are the way God speaks to us, right?

But then, the surprises. So much that I'd been pondering! The heart as being wise, tears, and the symbiosis between heartbreak and love...

That same day, I chanced upon something about Mother Teresa's "dark night of the soul." Thoughts and phrases that could well have come out of my own mouth! *Could it be I wasn't alone?*

Surprise—*tears.* I thought again of my elevator experience. Was that this *Joy* the guy on the CD was talking about, or something akin to it?

I learned that Joy was a central theme in the life of C. S. Lewis. This man of monumental intellect, who went from rock-hard, virulent atheist to becoming the greatest Christian writer/apologist of the twentieth century, identified the special phenomenon for what it is, and he named it. It affected him from early childhood and it was what finally led him back to Christianity. One of the great synchronicities, or meaningful coincidences, is that the great love of his life was also named Joy. (One might imagine a twinkle in God's eye when He arranged that one!)

Even as I'm writing this, strange coincidental happenings seem to continue. I'm finding books on Lewis lying around in places I don't remember putting them. And, right on the top of a stack of DVDs, was a DVD on his life I recorded a year or so before, had given only the most cursory viewing, and had completely forgotten about. I could swear I'd gone through that stack numerous times and never noticed it.

If that wasn't enough to make me think I was being led or pushed "somewhere," the very movie I was watching this afternoon had someone reading from Wordsworth, and the words *heart, joys,* and *tears* seemed to come out of nowhere. "Thanks to the human heart, by which we live / Thanks to its tenderness, its joys, and its fears…" and, "To me the meanest flower that blows can give / Thoughts that do often lie too deep for tears…"

Perhaps you'll understand my feeling that there's a mysterious "something" behind all this.

Heart, love, pain, joys, tears—why are these words and attendant ideas invading my mind so relentlessly? It's as if I've been, and am being, gently ushered along some beautiful, mysterious path.

It seems that this Joy is common to a greater or lesser extent to all of us—a sense of desire, surprise, and incalculable importance, and at the same time, as potentially humble and common as a faint, tantalizing whiff of a delicious meal coming from the kitchen upon arriving home from work. The closest thing to it in a more commonly-known experience would be, I think, the rather unearthly feeling one gets in déjà-vu. Just out of the mind's reach—teasing the consciousness…

Of course, that to which Joy points is truly indescribable. Lewis so eloquently tells us about a sort of pointing finger, if you will, and the ineffable object of that pointing can only be that One to Whom we pray. He likens Joy to "the scent of a flower we have not yet found" and says that in a sense, the central story of his life was about *nothing else*—that of an unsatisfied desire more desirable than any satisfaction.

As to my experience, if it wasn't Joy itself, this painful pleasure, as I would describe it, was certainly something *akin* to Joy in so many ways. One thing about the heart and Joy struck me as particularly fascinating: Why do our deepest sorrows and greatest rejoicings *both* bring tears? What an odd fact. That alone, I think, whispers to us of a marvelous mystery involving the heart.

CHAPTER SIX:
EPIPHANY!

The Surprise and the Connection

"Thou hast made us for Thyself, and our heart is restless until it finds its rest in Thee."

~St. Augustine

A near-palpable hint of a presence.

When I consider how everything came together, it seems almost magical and quite out of my control. Even the musical/lyrical engine that has been driving the phenomenon came by accident, out of left field, just like everything else.

I've been watching TV presentations of Southern Gospel music for quite some time now. Down South, it seems there are groups of gospel musicians and vocal artists who create a vast amalgam of fantastic arrangements and performances.

What's remarkable is that I'd never been even remotely interested in Southern Gospel music. It happened one evening as I was surfing channels, and I stopped for a bit on one of our family favorites, the Educational Channel. Something held me there as a woman came out of this big easy chair in the front row of the seated choir and began singing the final verse of "Rock of Ages."

There seemed a near-palpable excitement in the audience as she began to sing—and tremendous applause, as if she were someone very special. I learned later she was highly regarded in the field, almost revered. The chorus had what I can only describe as a sort of wild, free sound. I also learned later it was made up entirely of gospel music stars—soloists, trios, and quartets—a disparate group of artists who somehow blended beautifully.

The background music matched the quality of the vocal work—modern rhythms that somehow fit the old hymns they were singing, actually adding to the depth of the melodies and lyrics.

As the cameras panned over the choir, I noticed tears rolling down some cheeks. This emotion couldn't have been anything but completely honest and spontaneous. Surprised and intrigued, I watched the rest of the hour-long program. How attractive, this joyous combination of melody, background, voices! And the words—lyrics to which I'd never really paid attention before—what wisdom, what spiritual truths, what theology I was now recognizing in some of the old hymns! This was *praise!* Again, the Justice—"I know it when I see it..."

It was all of a piece: melody, lyrics, voices, background chords and rhythms—so many beatific faces, so many joyous tears.

Every Saturday evening, month after month, I'd watch themed-programs and specials centered around certain artists or groups, great musical arrangements. Such tenderness, such beauty! I learned from these programs the backgrounds of these people. To a man or woman, they seemed of the deepest, humblest faith. I was impressed with the lack of ego. No competitiveness—they all seemed to be supporting each other, cheering each other on. This was something I'd never seen, really, at least not to such an extent. So many, all pulling together, in one massive surge of praise.

But the truly curious thing was once again, the *tears*.

Not only did I often see them wiping their eyes and gazing up as if to heaven, it was happening to me. *I* was in tears, often really sobbing. Oh, not every song, sometimes only one a program (hardly ever the up-tempo, exciting stuff—almost always it was something more soulful, heart-touching). I never knew when it was going to happen, but it was happening at least once each program. I further found, since I was recording all of the performances, that it was the same song or songs each time I played that particular DVD. So many of the numbers would do nothing to me in particular. Some left me completely flat. Often, I'd go through nearly a whole program, then there it was. So strange, all of it.

I also had an almost eerie sense of something "just around the corner"—a sort of vague, sweet, undefinable desire—a longing, an aching for I knew not what. So strange. I realized I'd had this feeling or something close to it many times before and had always put it down to nostalgia. I somehow had the sneaking suspicion that though I'd often felt nostalgic, this was something that went well beyond that, and I'd never separated one from the other before.

Or, is some nostalgia (not sappy sentimentality, of course) something more than what we've thought?

So strange.

Equally curious was my "epiphany," brought about by a single word, uttered by a dear friend whom I'd invited over to, as I'd put it, "feed his soul." I wanted to share the music. I wanted to see what effect, if any, it had on others.

The interesting point is, it didn't matter what effect it had on my friend, if indeed this all had something to do with Joy. Lewis had described the *individual* nature of Joy—something unique to each soul, its only identifiable commonalities being, apparently, beauty, surprise—and something that breaks your heart, can bring you to tears.

So, enter another Paul. This one was nowhere near Damascus. He was in my living room. About halfway through one of the DVDs, he noticed I was wiping tears from my eyes. I think I apologized. I'll never forget what he said: *"I see the connection."*

Do you see it? Can you guess it—got a hint of it yet? How often the most profound can be the most simple.

A single word.

I didn't get it. Not then. It was sometime later, waking in the early hours of the morning.

Connection!

It hit me like the proverbial ton of bricks.

Connection—wasn't that really what all of it was essentially about? Communion, liturgy, prayer—connecting with God, the Author of Life? I was *connecting*! My tears had meaning!

This was the first crucial part of my epiphany.

I had desired to feel something when worshiping. At this point, though not worshiping, I was feeling, if not Joy itself, a kind of name-less twin, and there was a gut-level assurance from the context of the experience, the soaring words and music, the obvious joy and zeal in the faces, the very beauty and depth, the ever-recurrent surprise when it happened—that it had to do with God.

It was a short step then, to making this phenomenon, be it Joy or Joy's twin, an "engine" for the worship I so desired.

You can scoff at the simplicity of it or you can marvel at the profundity.

It was actually around two months later that I decided I would try "lifting up my heart", as they say in some liturgies, while in the beatific spell of one of those special songs or hymns.

I would pray.

I would pray *through* my tears. I would give thanks and praise. I would envision all the things I'd seen and heard of that made my heart bleed. I would beg for mercy for all His suffering creation, and I would plead for more compassion in myself, even with its attendant heartbreak and pain. Then I would thank Him for *all* of it. I would ask forgiveness for my many sins, on and on…

I would worship.

I settled into my chair, crossed myself, and started the program. My heart would be running the show from my end. My fondest hope was for a love affair with Him, heart-to-heart, as it were.

As always, I simply let that music, those voices, words, and faces—that whole ambiance of praise—wash over me.

As always, one of the special songs came along. And, as always, it began with a tear, and I knew something was starting to happen.

Maybe there was nothing special in what I prayed for in that first "worship session". Of course, I gave thanks. I have thanked Him especially for the tears themselves in subsequent sessions. I'm always wondering, *Is it actually going to happen this time?* It always has. (As of this writing, at least; I'm still in the fun house, after all.)

I prayed, as I imagine we all do, for a broken world out there and all its hurting creatures, begged forgiveness for myself and others, and so on…

What was different was the near-palpable hint of a presence. It was as if I was in a sort of bubble but wasn't really alone. I envisioned that veil between the spiritual and the temporal as a gossamer, undulating something that has no permanence—something that, unlike Him, is not outside-of-time, but rather, a phenomenon that will one day no longer be. Perhaps when the lion will, indeed, lie down with the lamb.

I was receiving, not in words but in feelings, impressions. Love, pain, heartbreak. Images of the abused and hurting invaded my mind—children, animals, the hungry and homeless, strangely accompanied by a rock-hard assurance of what I can only describe as *love*. I seemed to be giving and receiving love at the same time. My body alternated between deep relaxation and a gripping, pulsating tension. My mind swam with images. Faces of the hurting merged with sudden thoughts of our Savior on the cross. I wanted to *share* that pain, somehow, ease His burden. I thanked Him, again and again…

And then it was over.

Exhaustion.

And, as I look at what I've just written, I know I have failed. Just words. All I have are those very things I disparaged early on, when I said, "hearsay—somebody said it, somebody wrote it."

Words.

They've created dynasties and toppled empires, but as for my little bubble of whatever we might call it, they fail miserably.

Since they are all I have, however, I will use them to tell you this: I know what I have experienced and am continuing to experience. It may be unique to me, Jack-specific, or there may be multitudes who've had the same or similar happenings. I just know it was, and is good, a blessing.

And I believe with all my being that it comes from God.

And if it should somehow cease to happen, should *whatever* it is leave as unexpectedly as it came, I've been to the mountain. I've had a great gift for a season, worshiped the Lord "in spirit and in truth," and know those prayers have gone to and remain with Him in eternity.

How could I not want, indeed, need to share this? The message seems to be that not only is it available to all, but each has his or her own unique catalyst(s) for that Joy.

If so, and if you haven't come across yours, or have failed to recognize its character and potential, perhaps this little effort of mine will prompt you to be on the lookout for it. You will, I think, find it in something that has beauty, in something that breaks your heart. Tears will likely be a part of it, and it likes to come as a surprise. I'm still amazed every time Joy (or Joy's twin) appears. There will likely be several things that can actually summon it in your own unique experience. Will you recognize them and it?

Remember what the Justice said.

When you do see it, when you open yourself up to it—at minimum, it can feed your soul and you might just try adding prayer to the experience.

You may be surprised.

CHAPTER SEVEN

POST-EPIPHANY:(FROM MOZART TO A RUBBER DUCKY)

*More coincidences...the "mysterious 11s,"
outside-the-box reflections on this "Christian thing"
and "You, the Beggar"*

"Lead me not into temptation but deliver me from me"

~Me again

...that I might bury myself in You.

Whenhen I think on what I call the "Christian Dynamic"—the whole interaction between and among the elements of pain, Holy Sorrow, prayer and adoration, etc., the word *longing* comes to mind.

How does one become free of oneself, free of a world that is in what I would call "opposition by distraction" to the reaching of a true communion with the Creator? If we're honest with ourselves, we realize our spiritual poverty—we know we'll never really succeed in and of ourselves and that only that ineffable entity we're trying to reach can really do anything at all. Our job is to be open to His creative action. I think of myself as trying to steer a leaky little boat out on a dark and muddy river. I have a tiller riddled with holes and I'm just about able to keep my little craft pointed downstream, constantly bailing out the brackish water of ego and distraction. I have nothing to do with its propulsion. What moves my tiny craft and me is the current and mighty wind I call God. I can only steer a little.

And not all that well.

But I *want* more out of me. I *want* to truly prostrate myself, even if metaphorically, before my Master—my face in the dirt, acknowledging my poverty of spirit, my utter dependence on Him for every breath and heartbeat…

I think it's through our desire, our *longing* that we can lift our hearts to heaven. After all, aren't all activities and accomplishments begun with a desire, a wanting for something to be or occur? And how do we make the heart long to approach that Throne?

I'm back to pain and Holy Sorrow.

"Participate joyfully in the sorrows of the world."

~Patanjali

"Give humble thanks, my son, for a heart that can bleed for the sufferings of others."

~Anonymous

At bedtime, in my feeble attempts at true prayer, I'm learning to call up painful recollections of things I've seen or heard about in my life, those events that brought tears and outrage. Visions of abused children and animals, mass killings, genocides—the times I'd guiltily wished I could go take a gun to somebody for what they'd done to some innocent, some creature. And I recall the ache, the longing for things to somehow be made right, that the Lord would bring His Kingdom, His Second Coming *NOW* and end the madness…

One thing about pain and longing: they're real, pure, unadulterated by any distraction, to the degree we wish there *were* a distraction. I believe they can open the heart and let one truly approach prayer, however weak and minimal that approach may be. This must be what a dear friend, now passed, meant when he said, "Prayer is blood." I had no real idea what he meant at the time.

I think I get it now.

It's always a battle, at least for me. I often lose. It's not only the distractions and desires pointed world-ward that interfere. It's the Hyde side of me. The Dr. Jekyll-me strains upward, trying to capture that heart-pain, that longing. Hyde-me would have none of it, whispering all manner of worldly nonsense, telling me I'm weary, that I'm not "feeling" anything, that my prayers are going nowhere. Jekyll-me wants to dive all the way in, "break my heart and break my bones," as some pray. Hyde whispers that that's hyperbolic, draconian—even in metaphor.

The greatest selfishness is to become unselfish. The greatest gift to oneself is to lose oneself. It's all of a piece, isn't it? Humility, giving, loving, worship, prayer. Baptism, absolutely essential, also a metaphor for dying to become alive. All the mystery and majesty we cannot begin to comprehend, let alone adequately convey to those outside the Faith…

To lose oneself, to gain all by giving all—A great Christian paradox, among many.

You can't do it.

None of us can.

And I see I'm back to longing…

In my weakness and poverty of spirit, I can do one thing. I can turn my heart to God and truly long for what only He can accomplish in my life.

HE has to do the heavy lifting.

This *is*, I think, the Christian dynamic—the "rubber meets the road" side of the Faith.

(And this battle, I'm sure, will continue throughout my sojourn here.)

I "long to long". I have to believe that this whole action, this mix of pain, compassion, empathy, and longing will resolve itself into true prayer with time. God is infinitely patient. He propels my little craft and I, in my weakness, can only keep trying to hold a relatively straight course and avoid some hidden rocks and debris here and there…

Stories, poems, paintings, even music can sometimes create images that reveal what is difficult to otherwise describe. If you'll allow me, I'll try here to "illustrate" what I think of as true prayer, using something recorded in the Bible.

You're in this story.

You, the Beggar

You have a name, though no one uses it.

You're just "that filthy beggar by the city gates"—No one knows more than that.

No one cares.

Beggars are treated with disdain, even scorn. Passersby are as blind as you—actually more so. Blind in their hearts, unable to really *see* the lonely one amidst the chaos and the crowd.

Alone.

Alone. All your life has been spent in the isolation of this blindness, entirely dependent on whatever kindness might dribble your way in the midst of the commotion you hear around you. Dependent on whoever might deign to give you a coin or two, some scraps of food, a drink of water, any sort of shelter from the cold nights…

You are beyond embarrassment. Someone has to lead you away from your pallet to go to the bathroom, or you don't go, and you suffer through the day. *Everything* depends on others. You have no more control of things than an infant. You've never known joy, never shared a friendship, cannot remember the warm touch of a human hand (and who *would* want your lice?). You would like very much to die, but don't have the means to bring even that about.

The day is like any other. You sit by the path, hearing the conversations, the laughter, the arguments, understanding little or none of it. You hear an occasional coin land beside you on your grimy pallet. You try to imagine things to keep your mind occupied, but without any real experiences in your past, even that is difficult. Your only true companion is misery.

But conversations are different today. The incessant hubbub has a new flavor, a new sound—anticipation. It seems a teacher is coming. He'll pass through here on his way to Jericho. You have heard of this teacher. He's said to have been traveling throughout Judea and the Holy Land, working miracles.

Something stirs in you. Who can say whence faith arises? Is it a miracle in itself that you have this stirring of faith in this master who is apparently going to pass within feet of your humble pallet? Does the despair, the crying *need,* the many prayers you've uttered in your misery spill over into something that moves your spirit into belief?

The din around you takes on a new intensity. People have stopped their steady march to the gates and are now lining up on both sides of the road. You can feel the anticipation, sense the reverence for the One that's coming. You've heard them call him *Son of David,* the Messiah for Whom the Jewish nation has been waiting. The worker of miracles…

And for once in your life, this one tiny moment in time, you feel it: a faint hope.

You come to it tentatively, as if avoiding glass shards at your feet. To approach anything beyond despair is much like a baby's first wobbling steps.

He will only be a few seconds within earshot of your cries as he passes by, then gone.

Forever.

The crowd grows louder. The very air seems to have changed, taken on an ethereal quality. How will you tell when he's near enough to hear you? Will there be any change in the sounds around you, any clues from what they're saying or shouting? Your heart pounds and you're sweating far more than the hot sun on your head would demand.

One chance.

A miracle or continued misery until you die.

There is a change in the voices around you. Someone says, "There he is!" This is it. All of your life comes down to this moment. All the loneliness, the despair, the condescension and disdain, the insults—the heart that's been broken from your very beginning—all well up into that first deep breath and explode from the depths of your soul as you cry, "Jesus, Son of David, have mercy on me!"

"Shut the beggar up!"

But you cry out again.

"Don't disturb the Master, he's conferring with his disciples!" Yet, you still cry, "Jesus, Son of David, have mercy on me!" Someone jostles you, an exclamation point to their admonishment to stop, but you cry out again and again...

Anyone familiar with the Bible knows what happened.

...And the first thing you see in this life is the loving face of the Son of God.

This, I believe is prayer at its purest, most honest. It is possibly the first uttering, essentially, of what we now know as the *Jesus Prayer*. It comes from a humble place, born of our need, a desire to conquer our *own* blindness to our spiritual poverty. Something fueled by utter despair and somehow transcending it.

I want to be as that beggar. I want a violent prayer, as it were, to tear this longing, this aching need up from my heart and send it heavenward.

It will never be perfect prayer, considering its source.

But it will be honest.

I see His blood upon the rose and in the stars, the glory of
His eyes…
His crown of thorns is twined with ev'ry thorn
And His cross is ev'ry tree.

~Joseph Mary Plunkett, Irish martyr for freedom

I suppose this could be called the denouement or post-climax of my personal narrative. There is much more to be said, however, for those interested. I also want to tell you how to get the soul-stirring "Prayer of Sabeth," as well as "Waiting at the Last Stop" on YouTube, should you be interested, and I'll explain these in a bit.

Later, in Chapter Eight, there will be a series of four essays—my no-frills, low-rent attempts at apologetics that you may find of interest, as they provide some outside-the-box angles you may not have considered—also, potential ammunition, perhaps—should you be trying to encourage a faltering fellow Christian or prompt someone to explore Christianity.

It has been quite some time now since I discovered that singular potential for at least my own deep worship. You may be curious as to how my life has, after all, changed and/or benefited from the phenomenon. I think you may also like to hear more about Joy. I'll do my best.

I'll begin with the latter, as, truth be told, I and my story are of microscopic import compared with the whole concept of Joy and what it can mean to you, whether or not you find replication of my experience.

The best thing I can do at this point is to refer you to a place on the internet where you can play and perhaps download a great presentation I found regarding Lewis' Joy. The video is "Peter Kreeft on C. S. Lewis," and should you find it, you will be well-rewarded.[2] Lewis thought of Joy as the thread that brought him to God. It seems it's connected with beauty and is always an unfulfilled desire—a longing.

It points to God and the communion between your heart and God's heart, distinguishing it from usual or normal joy, happiness, pleasure, and so on. The thing is, you don't know what you're longing for. Your head doesn't get it at all, but your heart suspects it. I think of it as a whiff of heaven.

Again, the wisdom of the heart. It seems that in the rarefied atmosphere of this spiritual communication, the thinking mind seems

2   Search for "Vimeo Search" in your browser. In the Vimeo search window, type "Peter Kreeft on C. S. Lewis." Under the title should be "Highland Latin School." If using Internet Explorer, pick the *Advanced* Search Vimeo option. Be sure you're searching "Vimeo" and not "*Video*." Just click, and there you go. *As of this writing*, Vimeo's been free and these all work, but you never know with the Internet. You may have to play around with it a bit, but I can't believe all three search engines would change things.

to perniciously cause us to get in our own way. How interesting, the parallel with Eastern meditation ("no mind"). In both cases, but in different contexts, we need to get "us" out of the way.

Perhaps the most intriguing characteristic of Joy is this unfulfilled longing.

You might surmise, and you'd be correct in assuming that our Joy-triggers are unique to each of us. They can be anything from a majestic symphony to some childhood toy like a rubber duck, perhaps even a scent from something in the past. Have you ever encountered an aroma that called up a memory of something from long ago, even the ambiance, the "atmosphere" of a whole period in your past? Didn't it sort of bring up a kind of desire that was, in itself, a kind of mysterious, precious satisfaction, a not unpleasant ache for "something"?

Again, my efforts, now that I look at them, are grossly insufficient. It could be confusing. There is *so* much more, but hopefully, I've piqued your interest or at least your curiosity enough to prompt you to simply go to the website for Kreeft's presentation and/or get a copy of Lewis' autobiography, *Surprised by Joy*. Kreeft is the man to listen to on this, Lewis is the man to read. I actually would suggest Kreeft first, as his presentation is exclusively about Joy.

Now I can move on to something on which I *can* speak—my own experience(s).

"The heart has its reasons, of which reason knows nothing."

~Blaise Pascal

Again, I need to break in on myself here. I write on the fly, no outline or real pre-planning, and thoughts occur that beg expression.

In case some of what I have related makes me look like a "good guy" or some sort of "fine Christian," I have to quickly disabuse you of that notion. The best way I can put it is this: If a horizontal baseline were drawn separating negative below from positive above, I'd be lucky, by the time they plant me, to be very far to the north of negative.

My earlier life was full of enough bone-headed, two-digit-IQ self-centeredness to provide a good start on another book (think I might hold off on *that* one!). I was so abysmal I even messed up at messing up! No panache, just your common everyday birdbrain. If there is any comment I might deserve from you or other readers, the best I should hope for might be, "At least you've been trying here, pal."

So, how has all of this affected my life in the cold light of every day? What might have relevance or mean something in your journey? No lofty statements, but I do have facts, from some of which you may be able to find and pick some meaningful fruit.

Nothing much has changed, really, in my day-to-day life, with a few notable exceptions. For instance, I'm still nothing like a rigid Christian. Colorful language doesn't offend me much (providing it's not gross and/or truly unkind—or gratuitous, as some of modern comedians and celebrities vomit out to make up for what is often lack of talent). I feel there are far more important issues for not only Christians but for all people of goodwill to concern ourselves with.

As I said, there are some exceptions.

"Curiouser and curiouser..."

The mysterious elevens

Possibly the strangest change has been the increase of "elevens." "What are elevens?" you ask. Let me tell you...

For perhaps the past twenty years, my better half and I have been experiencing a most intriguing phenomenon. Separately, we each began noticing the number eleven coming up at various times during our daily activities: on clocks at home, the time and temperature display on a bank's sign when driving down the street, and so on. 4:11, 7:11, whatever. I really mean it when I say *separately*, because, for a long time, neither was aware it was happening to the other.

Sometimes, she or I might look at a clock to see what time it was. Sometimes, one of us might just happen to look up, and there it was. There were days it didn't happen at all, and I recall days it might happen many times to one or both of us.

Now, this might not sound particularly strange to you, but to put it in perspective, let's say you had a box of marbles with fifty-nine white and one black—the odds of one minute occurring out of sixty in an hour. You are blindfolded. You reach in to pick out a marble. How long might it be before you'd reasonably expect to pick out that black one? It could be days, even weeks. How about a second time the same day? Here, we are looking at up to five, six, seven a day, several days in series at times.

I've read this frequency is comparable to winning the lottery four to five times in a row. I don't know how big a lottery this statistician was thinking of, but the phenomenon is obviously far, far outside the norm.

My wife said she thought there might be a psychological element to it, such as unconsciously looking up at the clock multiple times during the day. But that would still statistically require many hundreds of looks to hit even five, let alone six or seven times. Plus, it fails to explain the numerous times I wake up during the night and see an 11 on my digital clock.

Please be clear: I have no interest in numerology and no concord with the occult, and I know my church does not hold with astrology and the like. I promised early on to relate to you my journey, and this is part of it. I give you facts, am being as honest as I can, and am resisting any exaggeration, the bane of many an overly-zealous writer.

One bane of *my* existence is insatiable curiosity. I asked a dear friend from Michigan what she thought. "Sonya" was known as one of the "Fools for Christ," a rather special person with some remarkable abilities and insights to whom I was introduced by my then-priest. (I think I'd like to be one of those Fools for Christ. At least I might have the "fool" part down!)

Sonya told me the elevens were simply God saying, "I am here." Works for me.

I also looked it up, as they used to say—now it's Googling. Coincidentally, eleven seems to be considered by many a sacred number in the Bible, representing divine intervention and transitional revelation, from Old Testament Law to New Testament Love. Do they have a special significance? You tell me. I only know they keep popping up. I also wouldn't presume to limit God's methods of communication in any way. That would be disrespectful.

I have since found that a friend and his granddaughter have experienced the same thing with the number eleven. I further found it's happening to a great number of folks across the globe. Check it out for yourself, if you're interested. By the way, no one seems to have a definitive explanation for the phenomenon. It seems "Eleven-ers" even communicate with one another online, have forums, and so on—and from what I've read, they are quite clueless as to what it means.

The reason I'm telling you all this is that the phenomenon has increased in my life, almost to the point of distraction some days, since that first "worship phenomenon" in my living room. Often there are days in series when I don't see them at all. Then they're back in force. How many times have I awakened in the middle of the night to see 2:11, 4:11, etc. on my clock? How often during the day have I suddenly looked up for no apparent reason and seen another eleven on the wall clock and thought, *Okay, Lord, if you're telling me something, can I get a clue here as to what?*

As is His way, silence.

There are other changes I have experienced. I'll list some here.

- LIFE IN GENERAL: It's been quite gradual, but I've had a steady lessening of interest in many "things of the world"—finding them somehow "flat" now and increasingly boring.

- SPIRITUAL RUMINATIONS are occupying my mind more and more.

- EMPATHY: I feel increasingly moved to pray for everyone: the "Good, the Bad, the Ugly," sinners and saints, souls, dead or alive, in heaven or in hell. Those I see on the street who I think might need a prayer for one reason or another—the unlovely, the physically challenged, those who are rude and off-putting socially. I'm moved to pray for those I read about or see on TV who've been convicted of heinous crimes, etc. Who needs prayer more than some of these?

- THE PHENOMENON OF JOY: Things that never moved me before are beginning to affect me. It's like God's version of an Easter egg hunt, except that He's hidden little treasures for the heart and, I'm sure, even Joy in plain sight and in different places for each individual, and instead of hunting them, we only need to open our hearts and recognize what He's placed before us. It seems that beauty can come out of nowhere in a rather rapid succession of events, or there may be long periods of nothing. There even seem to be *degrees* of Joy, at least for me. We can't make it happen, but we can be open to it, recognize it, and be grateful for it.

- MY HEART'S OWN JOURNEY: I'm trying to welcome that heart-hurt and be thankful for it. This is a challenge.

- CONVICTION: I'm becoming ever more convinced of the wisdom of the heart. My heart takes me in special moments to places of which my thinking mind never conceived.

- FELLOW CHRISTIANS: Interestingly, the more I ponder the characteristics of Joy, the more I can see that the business of the Christian is the business of dealing with that Christian there in the mirror. Just as Joy is unique to each of us, so is our Christian journey. The harder challenge is looking at others, no matter who they are or what they've done, as immortal beings, as special creations of God, period.

- CHURCH: I've found a church that is showing itself to be vital, vibrant, alive, with plenty of compassionate, energetic people dedicated to service. Our priest is humble yet dynamic in his quiet way, a true man of God. My communal experience seems to be benefitting from my personal experience, and I'm slowly developing a kind of thirst for joining others in prayer and worship, my individual devotion actually completing itself through a blending-in with that of my fellow believers. Worshiping as one entity, if you will, as the "Body of Christ"—His hands, feet, and eyes here on earth. I've finally come to realize it's not what I can get out of church-going, but what I can *give* when joining others in worshiping our Lord.

An interesting aside here: My new priest made me aware of Arvo Pärt (actually, though not a household name, the world's most performed living composer, I'm told!). I was taken to a new place by his *Da Pacem.* Curiously, the experience was not the same as with the Gospel music phenomenon. There were no tears, but there were colors, purple and blue, moving in increasing circles and dissolving behind my closed eyelids. I felt a profound sense of peace, as if I were somewhere above, if you will, the earth and all its gross concerns and interests. I felt I could stay in that state forever and know no boredom, no sense of getting on with life at all. How fascinating to me that this seemed to have no actual connection with the Joy (or Joy's twin) I experience with the Gospel music!

The only way I can describe the difference is by contrasting Joy with the "Peace that passeth all understanding" mentioned in scripture—where Joy is an *un*-fulfillment, the Peace would seem a fulfillment, perhaps even a bit of that of which Joy whispers. I only know that both of these extraordinary experiences, no matter what one might call them, were, and are profound. I also know I deserve none of this. It has to be some kind of gift, but why me?

Seriously.

Well, God works in mysterious ways, and I can only thank Him and wonder at His choices regarding whom He blesses. Since I know how little deserving I am of any of this, I have to believe *anyone* could experience what I have. Certainly, Joy is not exclusively available to Christians, even though it has so much to do with a sensing of Him in our lives. Just as God gave us (well, *most* of us, I'm tempted to say as I look around) a sense of humor, He gave us the potential for Joy. We were born with it.

I imagine what happened with the Arvo Pärt music could be a one-off. I've been rather hesitant to play the music again and perhaps find it was some sort of anomaly—real, but not to be repeated. That would be disappointing. I've certainly not had any sort of let-down with the Southern Gospel experience (up to this point).

Back to our list.

- THE OLD TESTAMENT: On that score, I'll take what I can get. Those sections that truly tie into the New Testament, the "types" pointing to the coming of the Second Adam, Christ, as well as the great founts of wisdom in those ancient books. I'll leave the rest to scholars and debaters.

- MY SENSE OF INCREASING SHALLOW-IZATION: Shocking! The more I see around me, the more nonplussed I become. Mention C. S. Lewis or Albert Schweitzer and you have probably a ninety-nine percent chance of getting the thousand-mile stare. Then try Kardashian or *The Bachelor*. Even something at the level of Honey Boo Boo eclipses most great thinkers in the public consciousness.

  I've heard of folks sending more than 25,000 texts in a month's time, and it's been estimated that most of their subject matter has about the depth of an oil slick. Substance-wise, we've truly reached bottom and are starting to dig (rim shot—sorry!).

  - Fact: Ten percent of the population reportedly believe Judge Judy is on the Supreme Court.

  - Fact: A woman has become a millionaire by simply feeding her face in front of a camera and putting it out on social media.

  [I worry about the *watchers*. What are we becoming? Actions and responses growing ever more mindless and just plain silly. We seem to be slowly turning into "robots" of a sort—folks have been worried about artificial intelligence (AI) taking over from man. What about another AI—atrophied intellect?]

- ONGOING: I think the heart sometimes drags the mind, kicking and screaming, to some hitherto unimagined areas. It is what prompts me to continue writing, and if the heart is indeed a "receiver" of "God-speak," as I've termed it, we need to recognize and embrace the wordless messages He's sending. Our souls need to be fed, and I have to assume it all, on this ethereal, spiritual level, comes from Him. To question that would be to deny one of the very premises of this effort.

I'm ever mindful that the heart on a more temporal level can be, to put it kindly, far less wise—so the discerning mind can never be discounted. Foolish is foolish, and I've been in that category often enough to not miss the distinction. It's only at that higher level that the heart seems to reign supreme.

- TOUGH TIMES: Interesting wording in, "All things work for good *to them* that love God." Interesting grammatically, yet somehow carries more gravitas, less flat than *"for those who..."* At any rate, believing this, there's nothing for it but to thank Him for everything, both good and bad, that happens to us. To thank Him for each heartbeat, every breath we take, and even be somehow grateful for the most horrific of calamities (*that's a tough one*), always keeping in mind that He's preparing us for a far more real existence elsewhere and beyond.

- VALIDITY OF WHAT I'VE SEEN AND EXPERIENCED: I'm ever more confident that what I've witnessed in the Gospel music phenomenon, this remarkable gathering of spiritually-sincere talents, is a true communion of hearts. Emotional, but not some juvenile, mindless excitement—rather, there is something quite mature that it offers, something deeply grounded in spiritual thought and experience, prayer, and profound worship. An earthly hint of "Choirs of Angels." Comparing this with what I've experienced with Arvo Pärt, I can see these two phenomena as microcosmic metaphors, if you will, for two distinct types of overall Christian experience and worship: the more "fundamental" of say, the Southern

Baptists, and the more liturgical of the Orthodox, Roman Catholics, and so on.

I see both as profound.

Christ is everywhere.

- CHRISTIAN ZEAL: "Steady as she goes," to use the nautical phrase. The level of enthusiasm for my journey seems to now be maintaining itself pretty much automatically. There are always troughs of course, but they're now expected and even accepted as part of the whole dynamic—they're cyclical, if you will. The ship always seems to right itself and I sail on.

Now some fun and miscellaneous musings—plus a bit of guilty indulgence in poetic impulses:

I think I can virtually guarantee food for thought in at least some of what follows. The curse and the blessing of an outside-the-box, maddeningly inquisitive mind is a plethora of thoughts invading it. Some *have* to be valid! Let's see.

Earlier, I made quite a thing about our lack of real knowledge and the fact that so much comes through the filter of man, an admittedly flawed and muddled creature. The state of the world stands as stark evidence of this, obviously.

I think I can illustrate, in a way, how much we rely on what *isn't*, and even necessarily so, if you'll indulge me here. This is really just a bit of fun, but there's a fundamental truth in it, I think. Judge for yourself: I can tell you that your car is not a car, and you'll end up having to agree. Let's say you pull up to my house to show me your brand-new vehicle.

You say, "How do you like my new ride? Isn't that some car?"

Me: "But it's not a car."

You naturally ask, "Are you nuts?"

Me: "Take off the steering wheel and what do you have?"

You: "It's a car. A car without a steering wheel."

Me: "Right, O wise one. Now, we divest your car of its gear shift. What do we have?"

You, in a bit of exasperation: "A car without a steering wheel and gear shift."

Me: "Right again. Now—we continue to disassemble this machine until we're down to a single spark plug. What do we have?"

You: "A spark plug."

Me: "Okay, when, at what point, did it cease to be a car?"

Of course, we now see it never *was* a car. It was a steering wheel, a gearshift, sparkplug, and a few thousand "and so ons." Even the spark-plug can be broken down into elements, all the way down to atoms, quarks, and who knows what beyond that. A universe infinitely small, it seems, as well as infinitely huge.

"Car" is a concept.

As is everything physical, and necessarily so. Without concepts, there would be no communication as we know it. We could not function. We would not be what we are, but rather, creatures not appreciably smarter than than the lowest bottom-feeders, even amoeba, blindly seeking sustenance from whatever we might bump into (although I admit to doing something like this at one of our all-you-can-eat buffets).

Just as interesting to me is the relationship between courage and fear. There is no courage without fear. The former is the overcoming of the latter! *Fearless courage* is an oxymoron. Taking this line of thinking to the extreme, one may do great things because of fearlessness, but true heroism is one being forced to operate *without* the fortunate trait of fearlessness.

I have no purpose in illustrating this, other than to remind you (and of course myself) that so much of life isn't always what it seems at base, and we often see things in the wrong light. The 35 to 40-thousand variations of Christianity might each contain some truth. Also, many may be complete nonsense.

Some writers ponder what one might term "mitigation"—positing that a Saddam Hussein or, I'm sure, even a Hitler or Stalin might be in less trouble than we might imagine in the eyes of the Lord because of how they *started*. Childhood abuse (as in the case of Hitler, at least), the influence of horrible role-models in their early years, twisted convictions that they were *right* due to propaganda, age-old handed-down prejudices, and so on, and so on. I imagine the tapestry with which God works in making His judgments must consist of a nearly infinite number of threads. Easy to see, in that light, the folly of our judging our fellow man.

Speaking of C. S. Lewis, I couldn't recommend his great book *Mere Christianity* more highly and enthusiastically. It is just what its title implies, and is one reason nearly all types of Christians love him and love his work.

In general, as I look ahead:

If you and I sit quietly, shut out all the hoopla, all the mindless input, the contradictory statements, and honestly consider the inexorable trends that are virtually ensuring our future, can you tell me you're actually optimistic? What Lewis once called a "cascade of nonsense" just a few decades back has become an avalanche. The economies alone, both here and worldwide, seem to just be borrowing (actually stealing) from future generations. Do you see that turning around? Where will we be in five or ten years? I don't have to bring up what seems to be happening to our very planet and all the rest…

Hasn't the ship sailed, really? I think it left the harbor long ago and we will soon be scanning the horizon over roiling seas and see, simply, nothing…

More than ever, I would think it has to become apparent to those of all faiths, as well as those of no faith, that any hope that can exist is *not* of this earth.

Christ gave us answers to the world's problems two millennia ago. Many Christians, as well as non-Christians, have said we're making progress overall. What I think I see actually happening, in addition to it all going off the rails, is a strange, gradual polarization. Wonderful, inspiring examples of sacrifice and compassion, heroism, tolerance, and so on, on one hand—cold hard bigotry, brutality, and stupidity on the other, with great masses of the generally apathetic in between.

My belief is that the more tangled the mess, the more confusing all of this is for the mind, the more important the wisdom of the heart becomes. To hear the true tones of that wisdom, just as one hears the ringing sound of a spoon tapping fine crystal, is to tap into that sweet something beyond. The wisdom to which I refer has to do with our lives "out there," something transcending the gross and mundane considerations regarding a civilization apparently hurtling toward an inevitably sad ending.

We were made for more than this. We are made in the image of God. We'll all die, but what of that? That's only a matter of when and how. What matters is the real "us" inside this fragile, gross shell and what happens to that "us" when we're finally released from it and can go home. Nothing else matters, not your mortgage, not your 401K, not even your health (which is going to go south on you eventually, anyway).

During this infinitesimal speck of time on the cosmic calendar, we have an opportunity to do those things that do count: love our family, love our fellow man in general, show compassion and empathy—seek a true faith, and then live it.

Him

Warm echoes in my heart—yet, a thrilling chill, music of
the spheres
muted trumpets, gold-girded angels—whispered, dulcet tones,
love song lyrics from a Master Scribe...

"Blessed are the meek…"

and I know the melody.

I have seen His face, you see,

hiding in plain sight, in the eyes of the wretched, the homeless,

there in the tears of the abused

I can hear, oh, I can hear His heartbeat in soaring symphonies

and feel His pulse in the low-down blues of the vagabond.

Gently, ever so gently

He whispers through the veil,

"I love you."

Joy

When did He regard His creature, this enlivened dust, and decide?

Knowing, all, He knew…

Weakness would ever haunt His creation, darken his days…

Was it at the first breath, or after that devasting disobedience that

left all in debt?

God gave a gift, wrapped in an enigma and tied with a bow

of mystery.

Did He place it under that tree, a subtle antidote for man's self-pre-

scribed pain…

Did He smile, giving us this Princess of Light, mistress of ache

and longing?

Always—just around the next corner as we stumble along.

Loving prankster, tantalizing—barely beyond the reach of our seek-

ing minds

but somehow illuminating dark places along the way,

Unsuspecting, unknowing, do we summon you with tears, or do
you bring them?
You ever tease, with those glimpses of God, always surprising,
never satiating
yet, your teasing, a satisfaction…
How strange.

Now, as promised, to "The Prayer of Sabeth"

Like so many of my experiences, I came upon the Prayer of Sabeth
quite by accident. I was surfing one afternoon and landed on one of
the religious channels. I had my thumb poised to continue when I
was stopped by the words I heard—a prayer, but yet somehow *more*,
like a beautiful poem as well. This level of humble submission, this
deep adoration and wish to "veritably die of love" revealed the simple,
yet profound faith of one who cut through all of it! No questions of
doctrine or creed, no real sense of a particular faith or dogma, none
of it. Just this little nun of a century ago, prostrating her soul.

I could not have been more affected by the very depth of it all—I
felt as if it had come down from heaven itself. I'd never heard anything
quite like it. It brought together the beauty of great writing and the
deep faith of one who was to become a saint. This "love song to the
Lord" is a rare work of what I can only call a matured and enlightened
soul, her devotion forged in the fires of her suffering.

I can only think "geographically" when I ponder such humble
devotion: how far, how many mountains and valleys I'd have to nego-
tiate to even approach such submissive depths.

I learned that the recently canonized Elizabeth of the Trinity was a French Carmelite nun back in the early 1900s. She suffered what was at that time an incurable disease and apparently wrote many of her prayers abed in her little room. To produce that kind of exquisite beauty when under such pain was marvelous to me, and I decided to record a narration of it. It would be truly ecumenical. Words written in French by a Roman Catholic nun, narrated a century later in English by an Orthodox layman, with a Lutheran Choir for background…

I began. I knew even as I made my first attempt that the music was right. It literally pulled me along, the nuances and dynamics just fit with the words, and my voice rose and fell with text and music in what seemed to me a miraculous blend.

I knew for sure it was right when I played back what I'd done. I can't speak for the narration itself, other than to say I often don't like to hear my own voice do much of anything, and this sounded perfect to me. As to the words of the little nun and the quality of the choral background, I've never heard a better match. As of this writing, if you simply go onto the YouTube search field, type in Sabeth (her nickname) and scan down the choices till you see the picture of a nun, with the title, "The Great Prayer of Sabeth", I think you'll see what I mean.[3] I have often simply let the narration lead me in prayer, praying along with her words. Should you choose to do that, should you say those words in your own heart while listening to that tender, near-sublime music, I truly believe you'll be blessed.

As to "Waiting at the Last Stop," I wrote, narrated, and recorded this in an emotional-level effort to encourage folks in my church to visit the lonely, oft-forgotten folks in care/nursing homes.[3] I also sent

---

3   "The Great Prayer of Sabeth" and "Waiting at the Last Stop" are also available on my website at http://www.JAXLayMinistries.com, click on the Inspirational tab at the top.

it out to activity directors in these institutions as a sort of training aid for newbies who might benefit from getting a picture of their charges as *people*—people who once had lives similar to theirs and who deserve respect.

"Both doubt and belief can be upward stirrings of the same goodwill."

…an invading thought upon awakening one morning

CHAPTER EIGHT:
APOLOGETICS, PLAIN AND SIMPLE

Christ, the Con Man
An Unlosable Wager
That Final Breath
Howd'ya Like Fifty Dollars?
Plus, "Might this be heaven?"

One can't lose, one can't win.

I am here including four apologetics essays. The first, "Christ, the Con Man," *actually* written to attract atheists, agnostics, etc. into reading an argument *for* Christianity, involved a bit of trickery. You'll see what I mean when you read it all the way through. The other three come at the idea of exploring Christianity from slightly different angles, all aiming to present an eminently logical reason for folks to at least look at something that could be of monumental, even vital import in their futures.

My idea of apologetics is more "It makes sense to look at this" than "You should believe this." By the very nature of our faith, we have to sound almost as if we "know it all" to someone we're trying to interest in Christianity. This is because we believe we have the ultimate answer to life itself, as well as to all eternity. We are told to "Go and make disciples of all nations." We have truth, and we are to spread that truth. Problem is, we can hardly avoid sounding arrogant. Phrases have become over-used, hackneyed and over time have devolved into clichés.

We need a simple, non-threatening logic, or attempt at it.

Though the heart can receive what I believe are special messages from God, He gave us each a mind and we need to use it. I truly believe we are crippled if only one is involved. If your heart should somehow tell you black is white, something is rotten in Denmark. The "imprint" I spoke of earlier would involve the heart, but one needs the thinking mind as well. We walk with two legs; we believe through two agents.

In a way, I think this goes back to what I said earlier about God not wanting automatons. He wants *thinking* Christians who love Him and love each other. Enough of these, and we'll have a great world. With the shortage we have now? Chaos. The fun house finally deteriorating into scattered shards of shattered mirrors and broken dreams.

Christ, the Con Man

They say, "If it don't make sense, it prob'ly ain't true." Not only does this Jesus story not make sense to us, we can call it utterly *impossible*.

Only three options: Christ was

1. A madman;

2. A consummate con man; or

3. The real deal.

Scratch the first one. Nobody with more than a room-temperature IQ, not even among His greatest detractors, calls Him nuts. He had far too much wit and wisdom, for one thing.

But option two? A fake, a con man. There we go. Let's look at just how impossible all this stuff was, and is.

We can really bring this home by putting *you* in Jesus' shoes (sandals), if you're willing. How about *you* being a con man for a bit? We're setting out to prove the man couldn't have actually done what He's said to have done. Either it didn't happen, or if it did, it was a *failure* of the first order!

As you take on the role of Jesus, remember: Whatever you say and do has to affect billions of lives down the centuries, inspire the building of magnificent cathedrals, the founding of universities and even whole new societies, the giving up of lives and fortunes—simply for believing what you tell them in three short years of ministry.

And, oh, boy—what you have to tell them.

The situation and the rules:

You're born relatively poor, or at least far from wealthy. None of the Jews around you are even remotely interested in a Messiah

Who isn't coming in some sort of magnificent, shining glory to free them from the Romans and fix their world. Also, you can only work with common folk: fishermen and so on. You have no bankers, no major CEOs, no radio or TV, no social media, no books, pamphlets, newspapers, etc. None of those exist yet. You're limited to just walking around and talking to folks.

As if those rules aren't enough, you also can offer them nothing of what this world values: wealth, power, and so on. Instead, you have to ask them to *give up* their lives in exchange for something they'll be rewarded with only after they die.

You have to walk everywhere in this hot, arid land without home or possessions and then tell a rich fellow, "Sell what *you* have and give to the poor."

You admit how hard it is to follow your teachings, how "narrow the road," and so on.

Oh, and by the way—you're God.

(You might try telling your wife, your best friend, your boss, that you're God—I'd predict a straight-jacket and rubber room by sundown. Here, you're saying this to folks who'd as soon stone you as look at you for this level of blasphemy.)

Just a few more rules: You need to talk them into replacing the satisfyingly vengeful "eye for an eye" with turning the other cheek and forgiving those who persecute them.

Okay. You've told them you're God, yet our rules say you have to ride into Jerusalem on a donkey.

You then must completely disappoint your faithful followers by not even defending yourself. After telling everyone you're God, you aren't allowed to do anything to save your own skin!

Then comes torture, ridicule, and…*now* you must tell some of your closest followers the same will be happening to *them*…

Finally, of course, you have to undergo crucifixion, the most horrible death the Romans could devise.

Many of your followers are now scattering like bugs.

Let's go back. This is a *con*, right? How do you, as Jesus, feel about this? You've made no money, gained no property, no possessions, you've disappointed and alienated followers, angered authorities both Jewish and Roman, been ridiculed, tortured, and are now dead. How did you do?

One might rightly ask at this point, "What was the payoff of this con supposed to *be?*"

I can almost hear you saying, "You gave me nothing to work with. This is nuts! No man could have made *any* success of this!"

Precisely.

This man could not have succeeded. This *God* could! The evidence has been here for nearly two thousand years. We number our very years by the time of His birth. No one has had a greater impact on the entire world.

History's most abysmal loser as man has won history's greatest victory as God.

Better consider, if you haven't, the third option I mentioned.

Eternity is far too important.

Don't blow it.

An Unlosable Wager

...from a letter to an agnostic friend

I'm heartened to hear you're becoming a bit more interested in spiritual matters. I've always considered agnosticism to be a pretty honest position. I think the word loosely means "without knowledge." One simply says, "I just don't know." You were interested in my journey, and it is interesting how it all came about. I think I discovered that it's not only the mind that comes into play with regard to spiritual things, but also very much the heart.

The only way I can describe what happened to me is by comparing it to the gut feeling you might have regarding, say, someone beating a child. You know it's wrong, just as you know goodness, compassion, and so on are right. I think, if it ever does come to you, it may well be that sort of knowledge, if that makes sense to you.

Certainly, I had the intellectual hurdles any thinking person would have, but in the final analysis, faith just came to *be* there, as though somehow planted in me. I had for a long time believed in a "Higher Power," actually God, but Jesus was the sticking point. I prayed for years simply to find the truth of it.

A great Christian apologist, C. S. Lewis, popped the intellectual bubble, and prayer seems to have done the rest, for I just woke up one morning believing! As for others, as far as logic is concerned, I can empathize with unbelievers, having been one for so many years. Those who look at Christianity, explore it, and deem it a load of drivel, I can understand. Those who don't look and explore it? I think they are foolish.

If someone comes along and says, "You know, there just may be a whole marvelous eternity available, one of incomparable joy, unceasing, beyond any earthly imaginings," why not check it out? So many folks say, in effect, "No, I'm not interested, at least not now—and maybe never."

Let's say one is strolling along one day and comes to a fork in the road. The path to the left sports a nice sign: *Promise of eternal bliss.* The path leading right has a sign as well. It simply says, *Nothingness (at best)…*

I cannot in my wildest dreams imagine any sane person not taking the path to the left, even if only to debunk what the sign implied, so he can go back and tell his friends what a load of hogwash he encountered and warn them not to fall for it.

I can't imagine why, but so many sane persons go to the right. What is it about the human psyche that causes rational men and women to simply go tweedle-deeing along life's road without any real concern regarding the most vital issues—their mortality and the potential hereafter?

So, if God exists and loves His creation, might He not look with more compassion upon one who actually explored, searched his or her heart and soul, and found Christianity or, for that matter, belief in God, Himself wanting, than on one who just dismissed it all out of hand? I guess that's my real hope, that you'll truly explore it.

Your books on comparative religions will likely treat all the prophets and founders of the various faiths fairly and equally, with many comparisons and similarities. The big difference they may ignore is that the centerpiece of only one of the major religions claimed to be the Son of God. That's the touchstone, I guess you'd say, the very heart and guts of the Faith. Either He is or He isn't. Nothing in-between. No "good man," no "wise prophet," none of that.

There's something called Pascal's Wager. Blaise Pascal was a French Christian philosopher-apologist from some centuries back, who in his less-arcane moments seemed to reduce the whole thing to rather mundane, even coldly logical propositions, and so on. I can't find his book right now so I'll just put it the simplest terms I can.

First, we lay the groundwork for this "bet."

The Christian believes in heaven and hell, whatever *either* might really be—as far from each other as the East from the West. The atheist believes in neither.

Death, nothingness, we will call "neutral."

Each is wagering his or her eternity.

Capsulized: Neutral is the *worst* the Christian can expect and the *most* the atheist can hope for.

Christian correct? Bliss. Wrong? Neutral.

Atheist correct? Neutral. Wrong? Misery.

One has everything to gain and nothing to lose. The other? Everything to lose, nothing to gain.

I'd bet with the Christian.

The purpose is not to reduce faith to a bet, of course. I think Pascal's Wager was simply an apologist's attempt to encourage someone to do what he considered the obvious: explore the possibility that there's something there. Eternity is far too important a consideration.

I can't say what you'll find in your searching. I only hope and pray that you *will* search. I personally believe that if someone truly seeks the answers, they will, in time, reveal themselves.

That Final Breath

...a confused apologist

There's a tombstone in Thurmont, Maryland that reads, "Here lies an atheist. All dressed up and no place to go." When C. S. Lewis heard about it, he simply said, "I bet he wishes that were so."

I've been pondering the near-glee I often encounter when I see atheists discount God, heaven, hell, the whole Christian package. I think they must be very brave. I tremble in my boots when I think of an eternity that would at best be nothingness, and at worst, separation from all light and goodness, as well as who knows *what* horrors (if some folks are right).

I would never presume to argue or debate with an atheist. I haven't the knowledge, nor, I'm sure, the wit requisite for the joust. My whole hope regarding anything I write is simply to encourage a good hard look at Christianity. My core belief is that the mind, the heart, and the instincts of one who assiduously seeks truth will bear fruit. What puzzles me is that non-believers seem so content and even sometimes rather giddy in their nihilism.

I could never be so.

I think there's something else with which the atheist could hardly disagree.

I can envision a scenario:

Two hospital beds, side by side. I am in one, our atheist friend in the other. We are in our last moments of life here. I would be a sad excuse for a Christian if I feared death. I fear the process: the pain, all the attendant mess of the body shutting down, and so on, but death itself? No. To me, this is the door to Paradise.

My real life is waiting, about to begin. I believe that last instant, that last breath will see me smiling, with the name of Jesus on my lips. But I wonder what my roommate will be thinking in those final seconds as his organs begin their final failures and darkness starts to settle in. Will there be a doubt, then? Will the scoffing, the witty derision still mix with his final breath? Might he then, in extremis, think, *What **if**? What if I've been wrong?*

The saying came out of one of our wars: "no atheists in foxholes."

How about deathbeds?

I've heard it: "Everyone has doubts." I've heard more than one Christian admit to the occasional doubt. Do atheists have doubts about *lack* of faith? They seem so arrogantly certain! I know this: I would love, should I able in those final seconds, to ask my roommate his thoughts as death settles on him. What does a man have to look forward to when his highest hope is nothingness at the end of it all? When the alternative to that nothingness, should he be wrong in his non-belief, is a horror, alienation from his creator—the realization, at last, of the paradise he's passed up and that he's facing a waiting hell, whatever its exact nature?

We can't debate the greatest of all questions. He can't prove a negative and I can't give him the sort of empirical evidence he seems to need. But how can he be *happy*? This, I would like some of our glib and witty atheist friends to answer for me. Forget, for the nonce, arguments, pro and con, God, the nature of the universe, the truth of the resurrection. Just tell me how you can so gleefully respond to the questions of life and death when your only belief is bleak nihilism and nothingness? If that's all *I* had to look forward to, not only in this life, but at the end of it, I would be one sad puppy, I'll tell you.

I honestly want to understand just this little bit of it. We likely have little chance of agreement on the larger issues, but to be so sanguine! Just give me your secret.

How do you *do* it?

Howd'ya Like Fifty Dollars?

Okay. A guy sees you on the street, walks up to you, says he's a millionaire and his hobby is giving money away. He offers you fifty dollars, no strings attached. That money could easily be counterfeit. You don't know the fellow, but you could really use the fifty right now.

Question: Do you take the bill and check it out, or do you just dismiss it out-of-hand and walk away?

I'll warrant you'd do what any sane person would do. You'd make darn sure that piece of paper was a fake before you tossed it.

I have just one appeal:

Atheist, agnostic, whatever—I implore you to just treat the possibility of Christ's being authentic the same way you'd treat that fifty-dollar bill. If you read or hear possible evidence of the falsity of the Gospels or the non-existence of Jesus, be sure of your source, your information, before you dump the whole business. Just make sure! Treat the possibility of eternal life with the same gravitas, the same seriousness and respect you'd give that little bit of money.

That's all.

I know I can't convince, per se, as I have no empirical evidence. We're in the deep water that has drowned even many a prodigious intellect on both sides of the Christ-issue, as far as getting an opposing position to budge.

All I can say is, I have tried to imagine eternity—and, of all the horrors I can think of, never-ending suffering, or separation from "all that is good" tops any list. Whatever we suffer here on earth at least has an ending! I just hope for you that when your final breath comes, you won't be recalling this communication and thinking, *Whoa! What if I've been wrong? I think that guy even described this moment in that essay!*

You see, I don't personally think (of course, I can't speak for other Christians) that the loving God I believe in would be prone to punish someone who assiduously sought the Truth their whole life and just couldn't come to belief. I can't say that for someone who looked a gift horse in the mouth and didn't even go to the trouble of making as sure as possible that it's all a lot of who-shot-John before walking away from what was freely offered.

How often in life are you offered a gift with eternal potential, one that costs nothing and you have nothing to lose? The only potential loss in this whole exercise would be in *not* accepting.

You'd check out the fifty.

Why not eternal life?

Some closing thoughts

"Preach the Gospel always. When necessary, use words."

~Popularly attributed to St. Francis of Assisi

When I consider this whole business of Christian worship and activity, one word sort of sticks out and looks me right in the eye and doesn't blink:

Work.

We work to help and encourage others. Outreach activities are work. Food pantries have to be staffed with workers. Ladies knitting mittens for the homeless are working. We work on ourselves, polishing and perfecting as much as we can, all aspects of our Faith.

Prayer is work.

Worship itself requires the work of concentration. The mind might spend a good deal of time in the work of dealing with doubts, frustration, disappointments regarding those around us, or events disrupting our lives, trying to maintain a Christian attitude. If one equates effort to work, the mental/psychological/spiritual gymnastics involved in *forgiving* in all sorts of situations apply. From deep, life-changing injustices on down to blessing those cretins who deliberately cut you off in traffic requires work, especially those favoring you with an obscene gesture to boot. Hard work, there!

Work.

Works.

"Faith without works is dead" as opposed to "Once sealed, sealed for all eternity." Can one lose one's salvation? I've always felt that though one can't earn salvation, it coming by grace alone, one could certainly lose it if one neglects works and thus has a dead faith. It's been said that we're not saved by good works, but *for* good works.

And, what of those professed Christians who blithely commit heinous crimes throughout their lives? Just for your consideration: *If* one truly and sincerely "puts on Christ" when saved, such abominations would appear to be impossible. Might not their salvation itself be a false one? Might they have been *not* sealed in the first place? Again, just saying…

And as I look at what I just wrote, I have to acknowledge that salvation doesn't mean we'll ever be anywhere near able to lead perfect lives here on earth. I think it does mean we work darn hard at it. We "work to do works," if you will—and we don't do good to become, but more, I suspect, because we *are* Christians. Lewis would very likely say it's the Spirit of Christ working in and through us, improving us, helping us up when we fall. I've certainly fallen enough. It's said that we all will continue this fall and rise microcosm/metaphor for Christ's coming down from heaven, on down into hades and rising into His Glory, living daily the Event of the Ages.

A bit more about "God in Hiding." Reading that the Roman Catholic Church was able to confirm the required two miracles and could finally canonize Mother Teresa, it crossed my mind that what *really* made her a saint was the fact that she soldiered on even when she believed God had abandoned her. Christ, in His manhood, felt abandoned on the cross but was never deterred from His objective, the saving of mankind. There is a special depth, I think, in this kind of love—to soldier on in bleak, black, perceived alone-ness…

On humor and irony

I believe God loves humor. I woke up chuckling this morning with a want ad running through my head:

> Sincere Christians wanted. Rumors of the death of our founder/proprietor are untrue, and we are in full operation. We provide eternal benefits, soul-health insurance, free instruction, and on-the-job training. Those allergic to work need not apply. Try Beelzebub's Boiler Room and Bar down the street.

And then there are the ironies. Christianity to me seems hardly designed to make one feel good generally, no matter what they say, although *ultimately* there are joys immeasurable attendant to being a sincere Christian. The short-term can be something else. Pretty much a challenge to somehow feel good when you look unblinkingly at all the misery in this world.

From what I've heard of the saints and what I've read of their journeys, the rear-view mirror is to be avoided. Even the good works one might do are not to be looked back at with much satisfaction, but rather considered in a forward-looking manner: *What have I not done as yet? How much more is there to do?* Love as a verb making *love* as a noun reality. Action creating substance.

Of course, God is not a bean-counter. As exemplified in the story of the ninety-and-nine, He rejoices over even a single victory. But we're human and naturally want more to happen. There is really never satisfaction, for the world remains a sick place, and sickness begets sadness. The only true satisfaction would require near-perfection, and we're not to see that in our earthly lives. When we consider it, God seems to be concerned with our efforts. The results? None of our business.

Speaking of earthly lives and the hereafter, it's interesting that some clergy speak of good works as putting "stars in your crown" and so on—as if heaven should be a goal for which to strive. I don't see that as the right way to look at the Christian dynamic. Shouldn't eternal bliss be almost a by-product, if you will, of a well-lived Christian life? Otherwise, we're doing whatever good we do to *gain* something, aren't we? Better we do stuff out of love and compassion, I think. Heaven will take care of itself (I think old C. S. might like that one).

There are many ironies, although perhaps calling them paradoxes or even Catch-22s might be more apropos.

Consider humility.

It has always struck me that, perhaps due to some mysterious "alchemy" or special dispensation from above, those few shining examples of humility I've encountered seem entirely unaware of it. I ponder the workings of such a mind. It seems a miracle. How to become humble? One might monitor oneself, one's thoughts, even remind oneself of past misdeeds and missteps to avoid pride and encourage humility, always telling oneself, "I've only scratched the surface of what's to be done…"

What happens? If one says, "I'm becoming humble," or, God forbid, "I *am* humble," that person runs the dreadful, even fatal risk of taking *pride* in his or her humility. There seems no escaping it.

I suspect the only way one can think about it sanely, and perhaps the best way to look at any progress or failure on one's Christian journey is this: "I'm on a road, a long and often arduous one, and I'm heading in the right direction."

That's it.

And, as proclaimed in the great hymn written by that former slave-trader, "Grace has brought me safe thus far, and grace will lead me home."

And that *is* it.

"Heaven goes by favor. If it went by merit, you would stay out and your dog would go in."

~Mark Twain

POSTSCRIPT:
SOMEWHERE, OVER THE RAINBOW...

One thing I can say, about which no one can disagree: We're all going to die.

Then what?

We've done our time in the fun house or, if you will, this learning center/Christian boot camp. There remain about as many questions as there are those to ask them. As Mother Teresa once replied to a query about what she'd say to Jesus once she got to heaven, "Lord, You've got some explaining to do."

Many have lived a "hell" on earth already, thank you. Debilitating, gut-wrenching diseases, the sorrow of losing loved ones prematurely, natural and financial disasters—all the rest. Even at best, dying under the least abhorrent conditions will be no picnic.

The one "out" of course for Christians is the Second Coming for which we've been waiting so long. Boy howdy, what might *that* be like? Party's over—cash in your chips, folks.

I ponder the "fear and trembling" with which we are told to work out our salvation. Just how straight *is* that path, how narrow might that gate be? If it requires, in addition to accepting His sacrifice and grace, *that* much effort for the hard-working faithful, what the deuce is the Second Coming going to be like for the lazy and apathetic among us who never saw love as being as much verb as simply noun—pew potatoes, as they've been called—those who never did "do unto the least of these"?

How select *are* the elect?

Might heaven be a more exclusive community than imagined—a sparsely-populated paradise off-limits to the lukewarm, the passionless, the lip-service Sunday-onlys?

Or is "fear and trembling" just a bit of hyperbole, and God far more forgiving than we've even dreamed?

Either way, whether He comes back during our lifetime, or we meet Him after dying and leaving this whole mess, we'll get our answers quickly enough. I'm sure some will be surprised, pleasantly or otherwise. I hope to be among the former, but I admit to the fear and trembling. I know how far I fall short, though I'm trying to give it my best shot.

Gospel means "good news." There *is* good news in addition to our salvation and the conquering of death. Where this world is full of heartache and pain, a new body is alluded to: it is "us" and yet not "us." The physical junkyard our bodies become as we age will be transformed into something quite unimaginable. Pain, depression? All of it no more. We may get the answers of which we've been bereft on the gross material plane. The *real* life beyond that veil has been promised as something the "eye has not seen," something of which the mind of man cannot begin to conceive.

If you're a Christian, you believe this, I'm sure.

If you're a Christian, you might stretch your imagination a bit.

I'll stretch mine here. After all, this little speck of time with all its madness and confusion may be something we'll not even remember in the golden afterlife. ANYTHING is possible with an omnipotent Creator!

We are said to be created for heaven.

My oh my. How personal that sounds, either way. And how exciting...

If it should be my own personal heaven, I might dare to raise my sights. I would be ecstatic just to see my Savior and prostrate myself at His feet. But what might "The eye has not seen and ear has not heard" really mean?

Boggles the mind. If we believe, as Christians must, that God is outside those old great frenemies, time and space, must we not, as "godlings" (as some have described a new redeemed and deified state) in paradise, *share* that state? One might envision, then, *limitless* potentials—and why not? What awaits might indeed put the wildest science fiction to shame.

Traveling through time and space, out beyond our galaxy, past worlds and stars, anywhere in the universe, just by *thinking* it. Endless sojourns in space and time at our whim! I imagine actually witnessing Franz Gruber picking up his guitar and singing "Silent Night" for the very first time on a snowy Christmas Eve in that little church nestled in the hills of Austria, perhaps the voices of those angels transfixing shepherds outside Bethlehem that night so long ago. My heart could burst at the thought of it.

How about colors we don't see here on earth, landscapes of a beauty unimagined, something our hearts couldn't even hold in our present state? To see, hear, touch, smell, and taste, at last, all that of which Lewis' mysterious Joy has been hinting...

And if this life is something we *will* recall up there, what wouldn't it mean to see loved ones who've gone before coming to greet us, even (dare I hope?) beloved pets some of us counted as family and mourned because we may have loved them more than we probably should have. (But who could help it?)

To walk, hand in hand, with many of those you have loved—down the golden streets of heaven, to dialogue with saints, to perhaps get answers to questions that have puzzled sage and mystic alike, and, above all—to be with Jesus, to hear His voice, see His eyes, His smile, perhaps lay your head on His chest...

And if it's to be only some, or none of the above, but, as promised, something far better than our little minds can conjure up, well, what can I say to that? I did my best.

Stay the course, friend, and you're in for a heckuva ride.

Oh, those words, sung so often without thought in my youth,
"As I rise to worlds unknown, and behold Thee on
Thy throne..."
to leave the binding, sucking gravity... all Earth's confusions
only a brief nightmare, ended by Death's awakening hand.
That old feared one, suddenly a friend,
no longer keeping cold watch,
but laughing like a child, loosing the tether,
releasing me as one might a red balloon at carnival.
One last look back and down
All those years, how many breaths—heartbeats?

Was it truly real, all that?

Half-whispered thoughts as I rise…

That madhouse below—was it real?

The hate, the greed, the destruction… Did we do that?

To each other?

Really?

Seriously?